SULTAN IN OMAN

During the writing of the *Pax Britannica* trilogy James Morris completed a change of sexual role and now lives and writes as Jan Morris. Of Anglo-Welsh parentage she divides her time between her library house in North Wales, her family home in the South and travelling abroad. Her best-known books are *Venice, Oxford, Spain* and *Conundrum*. She has also published three volumes of travel essays and edited *The Oxford Book of Oxford*.

CENTURY TRAVELLERS

SULTAN IN OMAN

Jan Morris

ARROW BOOKS

Century Travellers

Published by Arrow Books Limited
20 Vauxhall Bridge Road, London SW1V 2SA

An imprint of Random Century Group

London Melbourne Sydney Auckland Johannesburg
and agencies throughout the world

First published 1957 by Faber & Faber
Century Travellers trade paperback edition 1983
Reprinted 1986
Arrow edition 1990

© James Morris 1957

Front cover photograph:
Rebecca Ridley/Royal Geographical Society

Printed and bound in Great Britain by
The Guernsey Press Co Ltd
Guensey, C.I.

ISBN 0 09 972730 7

FOR MARK MORRIS

Contents

Maps

The maps were drawn by Charles Hammond

Introduction

The journey that is described in this book was, in its modest way, the last of the classic journeys of the Arabian peninsula. It was attended by few of the hardships and dangers of its terrible camel-back predecessors, for it was undertaken by motor-convoy, led by a competent Arab prince entirely within his own domains, and serviced throughout by industrious slaves. But like the greater explorations of the Burtons, the Doughtys, the Philbys and the Thesigers, it opened a corner of Arabia to the scrutiny of the world, it set a travellers' precedent, and it had its effect upon the course of Arabian history.

In 1955 the Sultanate of Muscat and Oman was a truly mediaeval Islamic State, shuttered against all progress under the aegis of its traditionalist and autocratic ruler. Few foreigners knew it, and nobody knew all of it, for its immense gravelly hinterland remained for the most part uninhabited and unvisited, and separated one part of the country absolutely from the rest. Our journey opened some windows into this remote and arcane place, but at the same time it admitted some momentous draughts: it was concerned essentially with oil, that irresistible agency of change, and its very accomplishment meant that the territory we were crossing for the first time was changed for ever.

The enterprise was also nearly the end of an imperial line, for in those days the British Government was still powerful in Arabia, and though I was the only European in those trucks, still the adventure smacked perceptibly of the open cockpits, Rolls-Royce armoured cars, proconsuls and spheres of influence of the Pax Britannica. The flag that flew above us was the red flag of Muscat: but the ghosts of Curzon and Gertrude Bell rode with us approvingly.

The Middle East in 1955, showing the relative
position of Oman.

Muscat and Oman in 1955, showing the
Sultan's route

1

Muscat and Oman—legal sovereignty—oil and the British—Buraimi—Fahud—the plan—'Greetings'

One fine Arabian morning in the middle of December, 1955, I walked into the palace of the Sultan of Muscat and Oman, on the shore of the Indian Ocean in Dhufar. Through the great gate of the outer courtyard I passed, and the slaves bowed low; through the gate of the inner courtyard, with the sea glistening beyond the wall; into the polished hall of the palace, lined with bearded and begowned retainers, their rifles in their hands; until there approached me from the darkened recesses of the building a small dignified figure in a brown and gold aba, a turban on his head, a sword by his side, a soft scent of frankincense emanating from his person.

'Good morning, Mr. Morris,' said his Highness the Sultan Said bin Taimur. 'I wonder how familiar you are with the map of south-east Arabia?'

I was not familiar with it at all, if only because that distant corner of the Arabian Peninsula remained the least known of all the Arab lands. In the atlas it was shown vaguely, a big brown sandy triangle, bounded by the Gulf of Oman on one side and the Arabian Sea on the other, a smudge of mountains in the centre, a howling desert around its perimeters: and it was marked, as if by somebody not entirely sure of his facts, 'Muscat and Oman'. Where Muscat began and Oman ended, the cartographer did not seem at all certain; and this was not surprising, for nobody else was either.

My frankincensed Sultan, descendant of a dynasty which had once ruled Zanzibar, and which had been in office since 1744, believed himself to be the lawful ruler of the whole triangle. He was an absolute ruler, and he thought absolutely. Dhufar, the southern coastal province, was certainly his; so was Muscat, on the Gulf shore; so presumably was the sparsely inhabited coastline, running around the horn peninsula, which connected the two. But the interior of the country, loosely called Oman, was a very different matter. It was a rough, mountainous territory, isolated by deserts and high ranges, inhabited by tough, unruly Arab tribesmen of varying degrees of peaceability; now squabbling with each other, now combining to repel some common enemy; owing diverse loyalties to tribal leaders and misty historical federations; often fierce, rapacious and xenophobic; many of them devotees of an Islamic sect, the Ibadhiya, which had died out everywhere else in Arabia. Was the travelled and urbane Sultan, a paternal autocrat educated in India, the complete and lawful ruler of these difficult people?

The British Government, which protected the Sultan's domains for him and largely handled his foreign affairs—in other words, which was still the basic power in south-east Arabia—was convinced that he was, and recognized him in its treaties as absolute ruler of both Muscat and Oman (as his title implied). Elsewhere opinion varied. The frontiers between Saudi Arabia, which controlled most of the Arabian Peninsula, and the various little states along the Persian Gulf had never been properly defined, and there were those who thought that King Saud of Saudi Arabia had, if anyone, legal paramountcy over the tribes of Oman. Moreover for many generations the Ibhadis of Oman had elected themselves an Imam, originally a spiritual leader, who had in later years acquired substantial political power too. The present incumbent, Ghalib bin Ali, apparently egged on by his ambitious brother Talib, had tried to set up Oman as a totally independent state, even issuing his own passports and applying for membership of the Arab League. In this intent he had won the support of the Saudis, who supplied him with money and arms and printed the passports for him; and of Egypt, the most powerful indigenous force in the Middle East, whose rulers were dedicated to the eradication of all western influence in the Arab world, and who therefore preferred a chauvinistic Imam to a reasonably Anglophile Sultan. Their case was perfectly arguable. In 1913 many of the tribes of the interior had rebelled against the Sultan's authority and had fought a fairly successful war against him. The agreement which concluded it, called the Treaty of Sib, had pledged the Sultan not to interfere with the internal affairs of Oman. Could he still be its legitimate sovereign ruler, with such a limitation on his authority? At the time of the treaty some British observers believed it to establish, in effect, two separate states: and the Imam agreed with them.

Forty years later the British might not have been very interested, were it not for oil: but the search for new oilfields at that end of the Arabian Peninsula revived the whole vexed question of frontiers and allegiances. Higher up the Persian Gulf the demarcation lines between oil concessions were well defined and generally recognized; but the hazy frontier between Saudi Arabia and Oman, the subject of innumerable diplomatic skirmishes, became an economic battle line. For years an American company had been active in Saudi Arabia, bringing that antique autocracy immense wealth and considerable political power; and if Oman could be brought legally within the Saudi orbit, any oil there might also be exploited by Americans. However, the Sultan had already (*pace* the Treaty of Sib) granted a concession for the whole of Muscat and Oman to a predominantly British company; and though his right to do so was disputed by the Imam, the Saudis, the Egyptians, and many an American oil lawyer, the British Government was supporting him strongly. The truth was that the future of the Persian Gulf oilfields might govern the destinies of Great Britain, and it seemed vital that any new oil deposits should be controlled by sterling companies. Indeed, according to an article in the *New York Times* at about that time, 'whoever controls these new sources of oil may control the main sources of energy of the world until atomic energy becomes available.' To achieve this the British were even willing to risk antagonizing the Americans, and Whitehall backed the Sultan and the British oil men with an uncharacteristic force and decision.

The most important gateway to these regions was a group of oases called Buraimi, deposited on the junction between Saudi Arabia, the Sheikhdom of Abu Dhabi (linked to Britain by treaty), and the Sultanate of Muscat and Oman. The sovereignty of this place was not very clearly defined. The British claimed it on behalf of the Sheikh and the Sultan, each of whom thought himself ruler of part of it. The Saudis claimed it for themselves. A straggling series of palm groves and villages, Buraimi was a centre of communications and political activity: the power that controlled Buraimi was in a fair way to controlling all that part of the frontier. Through it passed the Imam's gold and arms from Saudi Arabia, and the Saudis did their best to suborn officials stationed there. According to the British, one man was offered £20 m. to declare for King Saud (a figure taken by most people with a slight but sympathetic pinch of salt) and largesse was certainly distributed widely among the local tribesmen. In 1952 the Saudi Government, using transport provided by the American oil company, sent forces into the oasis and occupied part of it. The angry Sultan was restrained from marching against them by the British Government, which did not then want to endanger relations with the United States; but arbitration failed, and in 1955 the British themselves expelled the Saudi forces. When I arrived in south-east Arabia Arab troops under British command and control occupied Buraimi firmly and unblushingly; and *de facto* sovereignty was undeniably held by the Sheikh and the Sultan.

The world, watching these events, and observing the protracted diplomatic squabbles which accompanied them, generally assumed that Buraimi sat bang on top of a fabulous oilfield. In fact, the oil companies and the governments had their eyes chiefly on country away to the south-east. Buraimi was a key to this region: but to the oil prospectors the magic word—a name on a large-scale map, no more—was Fahud. Where the Empty Quarter of Arabia met the Oman highlands there was a wide semi-desert plain, speckled with sparse shrubbery, inhabited only by poor nomads: a country of gazelle and oryx, where even the cheetah had been seen. In these steppes stood a small symmetrical cirque of hills, pierced by one narrow pass, which seemed to the geologists to offer chances of very great oil strikes. It was called Jebel Fahud. The oil company had established a small camp outside the cirque, and was taking material there by air and by truck across the desert from the southern coast. Soon the drillers would begin work. It was an exceedingly isolated spot, hardly visited by Europeans before: when I flew over it, on my way to Dhufar, all I could see was a speck of huts, an airstrip, and a converging mesh of lorry tracks running in from the desert. But it lay on the edge of territory remoter still. The Fahud country was inhabited by the Duru tribe of Bedouin, who had not subscribed to the Treaty of Sib, and who would therefore find it difficult to contest the concession, even if they knew how to; but the entire mountain range which overlooked it was under the authority of the Imam. It was, moreover, a place of notorious turbulence and ill-will. The oil company had been obliged to help the Sultan to finance a new private army, the Muscat and Oman Field Force, to protect its interests: and it was distinctly chary of continuing the work with the political future of the country so unsettled. By the summer of 1955 there was a real possibility that the Imam might join forces with his friends the Saudis, and that the oil concession would at best be difficult to maintain and at worst lost altogether to the Americans (quite apart from the fact that until the sovereignty of Oman was determined the legality of the Sultan's concession could always be questioned). To the British Government this was a most disagreeable prospect. First, a great strike at Fahud could do much to shore up the rickety British economy. Secondly, the War Office planners, deprived of most of their Middle East strong-points, were especially interested in Oman oil because it could be piped directly southward to the Indian Ocean, avoiding the strategic dangers of the almost land-locked Persian Gulf. Thirdly, the whole British position in the Gulf area, maintained chiefly by a series of treaties with local chieftains, was being threatened by just such Egyptian and Saudi intrigue as the flirtation of those Powers were conducting with the Imam. The British authorities, though they disliked talking much about their associations either with the Sultan or with the oil companies, were in fact excruciatingly concerned with the situation in Oman.

Nor could the Sultan view it with the aloof and unruffled equanimity expected of such Oriental magnates. He was not a rich sultan, as sultans go. His father had been harassed by severe financial troubles, and he was trying to retrieve the state fortunes by careful husbandry. A half-share in Fahud oil deposits might, with luck, make him one of the richest men on earth, and his sultanate one of those little kingdoms whose decisions send a shiver around the treasuries of the world. (The Ruler of Kuwait was already the principal single provider of new money for the London investment market.) Moreover, oil apart, the Sultan naturally did not like the idea of a separate kingdom, under foreign patronage, arising within the territories that were his by heredity. He had never been to Oman, but his family sprang from the interior, and his views were therefore at once economic, political and faintly sentimental. Unlike the cartographer, he had very pronounced views on the relative positions of Muscat and Oman: both were his.

So one day the Sultan, the British Government and the concessionary oil company (perhaps in that order, perhaps not) decided that the time had come to settle the matter once and for all. The oil men were nearly ready to begin drilling in the Fahud cirque. The seizure of Buraimi had, for the moment, quietened the frontier, both the Saudis and the Americans being rather taken aback at so forcible an expression of British policy. The sterling economy was shaky, and all over the Middle East Egyptian and Communist propaganda, allied often with Saudi gold, was nibbling at the British position. Even the need for a joint Anglo-American policy towards the Arabs seemed to the British less important than the need for new oil resources in stable, friendly territory. As for the Sultan, his four separate private armies were now in good shape under their British commanders, and he had already taken over one or two villages, on the edge of the highlands, whose status, allegiance, opinions, value and intentions all seemed equally obscure. The stage was set. In conditions of elaborate secrecy, plans were completed for the Sultan to impose his authority by force upon the inner mountains of Oman.

Only half a dozen Europeans had ever visited those fast-nesses, and even fewer had ventured into the more fanatically xenophobic of the villages. Very little was known about the country. Traders, it was true, did take their wares down to Muscat; there were regular camel caravans from the moun-tains to the coast: some distinguished English explorers had produced rudimentary maps; aircraft had flown over the range. Politically, though, the region was more or less blank. The local officials were all appointed by the Imam, and the Sultan's soldiers, judges, administrators, tax-collectors and teachers had no writ there. The early European explorers had penetrated the mountains with the Sultan's blessing, in the days when his authority was supreme in Oman; but the more recent ones had run a decided risk of extinction, and had sometimes travelled in disguise. The Sultan's strategy, of British inspiration, was therefore carefully considered. Recon-naissance flights were made over Nizwa, the Imam's capital; the Muscat and Oman Field Force, with its British mercenary officers, was concentrated at Fahud; on the coastal side of the mountains, in Muscat, the Batinah Force (another private army) was alerted. Links were established with friendly leaders in the interior, and a slight *coup d'état* was encouraged in one of the most influential tribes. Wavering dignitaries were enticed to Dhufar, where they were handsomely entertained and sometimes given new rifles as suggestive mementoes. The friendship of the Bedouin on the edge of the mountains was consolidated. It soon became apparent, thanks to such preliminary whittlings and subterfuges, that the Sultan was planning a campaign.

The scheme was to advance upon Nizwa from the west, driving the Imam and his supporters into the high mountains that lay between that citadel and the sea. If he tried to escape by either of the two practicable passes over the hills, his way would be blocked by the Batinah Force, which would also have disposed of any enemies on the coastal side of the range. Radio communications were arranged; airstrips were made ready; a pair of clumsy mountain howitzers was acquired; the soldiers looked forward to a healthy old-fashioned little war. But so strong were the Sultan's forces by the standards of south-east Arabia (where, indeed, everybody went armed, but generally only with elderly and erratic rifles) that it seemed very unlikely there would be much resistance, when it came to the point. In some ways the Omani mountains were among the most backward places on earth, where never a truck had been seen, nor a telephone rung, nor even a machine-gun chattered: the mechanized column of the field force would, no doubt, have an instant and profound moral effect. So at the same time plans were laid for the Sultan to make a triumphant and dramatic motor journey through his domains, to ride in triumph through his own modest Persepolis. Before the last echoes of the fighting had eddied away through the hills, he would set out secretly from Dhufar across the great gravel desert called the Jaddat al Harasis, an unknown waste. Then he would travel north along the oil track to Fahud, and suddenly, all unexpected, pounce into the mountains to receive the salutations of his defeated enemies. At Buraimi he would solemnize the restoration of his sovereignty there by a ceremonial meeting with his colleague the Sheikh of Abu Dhabi; and finally, crossing the hills, he would journey down the Gulf coast for a victorious entry into Muscat, his capital, so demurely tucked away in rocky coves that the old Greek navigators called it 'the hidden port'.

This journey had never been made before, least of all by motor vehicle. No such crossing had been made of the Jaddat al Harasis; nobody had driven from Dhufar to Muscat; the mountains of Oman were almost unexplored; even the Wadi Jeziz, the pass between Buraimi and the sea, had (until a few years before) been described only by the hardiest of Arabian travellers. Taking a truck from Dhufar to Muscat would, for the first time, prove it possible to drive the whole length of South Arabia, from Aden to the Gulf of Oman. It would not be a journey comparable to the old Arabian travels, month upon month of perilous camel-riding, plagued by climate and hostility, such as the great explorers of Arabia had undertaken in the past; but it would be blazing a trail still, and a remarkable royal progression.

So it was that early in December I found myself at Salala, capital of Dhufar, asking permission (in a letter of ornate rectitude) to accompany the Sultan on his adventure. The campaign in Oman was about to begin; we had no news yet from the interior; but one evening there arrived for me the following note from the palace, typewritten by the Sultan himself on blue crested writing paper:

Greetings. I have your letter of today's date and I thank you for your kind congratulations.

I was about to write you when your letter arrived. I am pleased to inform you that you are permitted to accompany me on my journey to Oman. Your interest to write an account of my journey is very much appreciated and hope you will have a pleasant and comfortable journey.

Will you please be ready to leave on Monday the 19th December at about 1.45 p.m.

SAID BIN TAIMUR

2

Dhufar—the askaris—Salala—Qara mountains—
tea with the wali—the abyss—'better than the Backs'—
strange people—good news—to the palace

In the meantime I was free to explore the delectable province of
Dhufar—or almost free. For many years there had been a
Royal Air Force landing ground outside the village capital of
Salala, and an American oil company was drilling (unsuccess-
fully) along the coast: but to that day no foreigner might
wander about without the escort of one of the Sultan's armed
askaris. My memories of Dhufar are thus coloured by the
ubiquitous presence of these agreeable little men. They were
mostly natives of Aden or the Hadramaut, all very small, and
very agile, and very affable; their beards were black and bushy;
their smiles were broad; their customary method of greeting
was a sudden raising and lowering of the eyebrows, meant to
convey diffident friendly messages, but to the westerner infinitely salacious in style. The askaris wore indeterminate turbans
over long loose gowns, heavy with bandoliers and curved daggers, and when they hastened barefoot over the ground they
did so with a strangely attractive trotting motion, as if they had
goats' hooves.

At the landing ground, where the R.A.F. were my hosts,

these gnome-like watchmen occupied quarters near the entrance, and sat through the long waiting to ensnare some ill-informed passer-by for an interminable cup of coffee and an hour or two of unintelligible badinage. At night they were dispersed through the camp, canes and old Martini rifles clutched in their hands, so that when you went to bed you would find a couple of them happily encamped upon your doorstep: and sometimes, in the middle of the night, you would hear one singing a love-song to himself—first a deep, throaty, rumbly kind of voice, natural to the askaris, and then a shaky and timorous falsetto intended to represent the quavering responses of the virgin. (The Somali tribesman in Africa also converses with himself in different voices, but not simply for fun or for company in the long night; he chatters away in three or four separate characters to convince any prowling enemies that a horde of confident warriors is ready to repel an attack.) The askaris were always alert and always eager. 'Askari!' you would bawl, as you drove through the gates in the morning; and out would tumble two or three smiling little men, fastening their bandoliers and brandishing their rifles in sprightly competition for the pleasure of accompanying you.

One or two other mild restrictions governed your activities in Dhufar. You must not smoke in public, for tobacco was forbidden by the pious Sultan (though by no means unknown). You must not drink alcohol in public, for strong liquors were banned everywhere except in the R.A.F. camp. If you wanted to take photographs, you must do so from inside your car. Dhufar was a little backward Paradise on the sea-shore, and the Sultan (who ran it like a private estate) did not want to see it contaminated.

For anyone who imagined Arabia as one vast sand desert, Dhufar offered an entrancing surprise. Deserts indeed surrounded it, but the province itself consisted of a mountain range running down to the sea in the east and the west, and enclosing a wide and green crescent-shaped plain. This place had once formed part of the Incense Coast, so celebrated by the ancient geographers, and had sustained a rich and talented Sabaean civilization: the frankincense grown on the inland side of the hills had been the foundation of many a wealthy merchant house, and had been shipped through Dhufar to innumerable distant and exotic markets. (It grew there still, and almost the only artistic products of the province were small, drab incense burners of a yellowish clay.) This was perhaps the most favoured part of the whole Arabian Peninsula. By a climatic quirk the monsoon just touched that particular corner of Arabia, and the foliage was therefore lush and semi-tropical. Along the coast were groves of coco-nut palms and vivid fields of sugar cane, plantains, wheat, millet, indigo and cotton. Across the plain of Jurbaib, behind Salala, ran two fresh and virile streams to water the crops and gardens of the capital. Here and there was an old irrigation well, and two aged camels walked round and round it stolidly, urged by a gleaming bare-backed negro, with a creaking of warped wooden devices and harnesses, and a bubbling of water, and a clanking and clashing of the buckets. The plain was gentle, and littered with monuments: here was the immense long tomb of some forgotten divine, twenty or thirty feet from end to end, with upright stones to mark its extremities; and here a huge shapeless pile of rubble was all that remained of the pre-Islamic city of Balid. There were no roads in Dhufar, but good rough tracks ran along the coast and into the hills, and beside them stood many a bearded ancient, his rifle across his shoulders, trying to thumb a lift into Salala.

It was no rich metropolis, the provincial capital of Dhufar, but an unpretentious group of three villages infused with a most restful calm. In its centre stood a prominent group of tall square buildings: from the distance they looked like skyscrapers, and they were decorated rather in the style perfected by the Nabateans at Petra; but they were poor, tumble-down structures when you reached them, with no claims to grandeur. The prosperous incense traders had left Dhufar long before,

and Salala was now no more than a market town, a modest
port, and the Sultan's Balmoral. A strange mixed community
wandered through its streets. There were Arabs of several
different tribal origins: the men, though small and thin,
moving with a certain proud dignity; the women, severely held
in check, veiled with a hideous and alarming black beak-like
mask, stiff and stifling, which gave them an air at once theatrical and pathetic. Then there were the slaves and freedmen—
strapping black men, plump and well-clothed, with blank un-
lined faces; their wives went free and unveiled, and often
darted out of their palm-frond houses to see the passers-by,
immensely vivacious and flirtatious, and jingling with orna-
ments. Dark-skinned hillmen wandered in from the mountains, carrying sticks and wearing nothing very definable, their
hair fuzzy and their eyes gleaming. A myriad children ran
about the alleys chattering, the uncircumcized boys sometimes
stigmatized by a grotesque shaving of their heads, upon which
only a tall cockscomb of hair was left standing in the middle like
an ape's. Khaki-clad soldiers were occasionally to be seen (in
their camp outside the town you could hear them practising the
Morse Code on whistles); and sometimes a splendid Bedouin
chieftain from the interior stalked through with a company of
followers.

But the palace dominated the place, like the castle at Wind-
sor or the Mormon Tabernacle in Salt Lake City. All these seaside capitals of eastern Arabia had their big fortress-palaces in
which the ruler reclined among his dependants and syco-
phants, his outlook, like his creature comforts, generally
depending upon the size of his oil royalties. Kuwait's was the
grandest; Bahrain's the most stylish; Doha's the most horrible;
and Salala's probably the nicest. It stood directly on the sea-
shore, a long crenellated building, surrounded by high walls
and complicated by connecting courtyards and alley-ways. A
wide avenue of palm trees led to the double gate-tower at its entrance. In a window above the gates a bearded Sikh in a white
turban could often be seen surveying the scene before him or

contemplating a chess problem: he was the Sultan's state engineer. Sometimes a little Indian in a battered trilby hat drove through the gate in a truck: he was the Sultan's mechanic. Every Tuesday morning a slim young Englishman in uniform marched out of the palace after his weekly conference with the ruler: he was the commander of the Dhufar Force, the Sultan's local army. Muscular, well-armed slaves guarded the gateway to the palace; and in one corner of it stood the prison, where Dhufar's entire criminal population languished. ('These are our murder records,' confided an official at Scotland Yard when the Sultan paid a visit to London. 'I expect you have the same kind of problems at home?' 'Let me see,' said the Sultan, turning to his aide, 'when *did* we last have a murder? Was it before or after the war?')

A little way down the coast the Sultan had a garden palace, and this I remember with delight as symbolic of the voluptuous lushness of Dhufar. It is not often in modern Arabia that the environment echoes that poem of Walter de la Mare's:

> *Sweet is the music of Arabia*
> *In my heart, when out of dreams*
> *I still in the thin clear murk of dawn*
> *Descry her gliding streams*

—but here the words occurred to me deliciously, perfectly attuned to the setting, as I lay one morning in the pool outside the little white palace. The mountain water ran all about me, cool and tingling. The garden was full of the scent of flowers, sharpened by a *soupçon* of the smell of burning wood from some peasant fire outside the walls. Beyond the palm trees a white-sailed dhow sailed by, bringing dates from Muscat (there are no date-palms in Dhufar). My askari sat cross-legged upon the bank, smiling and picking his crooked teeth with a twig; sometimes an animal noise floated in on the breeze—a camel's cough, a bird, a rustling in the grass; and beneath the coco-nut grove in front of me an old husbandman was deftly shelling

26

coco-nuts with a hatchet, now and then limping over with a holed nut and inviting me to taste its milk. I felt like some poor duped traveller of fable, lapped in wine and honey but about to be converted (it seemed inescapable) into a swine.

The hinterland was hilly, and because of the miracle of the monsoon, parts of these Qara mountains were dressed in green meadows, with generous foliage, flowers, flocks of rich cattle, and tribes of strange non-Arab peoples, often living in caves, almost naked, speaking languages of their own and maintaining their own obscure manners and customs. There were several of these tribes, but the most powerful of them seemed to be the Qara people who had given their names to the hills (though locally the range was called the Shahara, after a once-potent tribe now relegated to menial obloquy). Only a few tracks led into the mountains, and one or two passes pierced them; but often the tribesmen were to be seen in Salala or on the plain. The author of *Periplus of the Erythrean Sea*, writing in the first century A.D., described Dhufar as 'a mountainous country, hard to cross, wrapped in thick clouds and fog': and indeed during the monsoon the mountains were totally enshrouded in cloud, and a thick pall hung low over Jurbaib, veiling Salala in mist; aircraft approaching the landing ground had to skim in low over the sea, and ships could not unload at Risut or Salala. For a month or two before this period of obliteration the Qara people emerged *en masse* from their mountains, bringing their cattle with them, their shields and their sticks, their few poor clothes, their indigo-stained faces, their immemorial prejudices. Then the plain was full of these queer stone-age figures, lean and handsome, and they wandered like fauns through the little market-place of Salala, where the negro women squatted on their haunches beside their pans of beans, and a stench of fish lingered on the air.

At other times of the year, though you might see a few hillmen in Salala, you could drive into the foot-hills of the mountains without passing any at all, but haunted by a feeling that from rocky holes and crannies high above many a keen dark eye was observing you. One day I crossed the plain and wandered up a narrow cleft in the mountains to a glen bubbling with streams and pools. It was a confined, cylindrical, dark, secret kind of place. High cliffs surrounded it on every side; pale sun-dried grasses lined its floor; in the biggest of the pools, deep and clear, hundreds of small minnow-like fish swam languidly. There was not a soul to be seen, nor any sign of habitation; but one of the snakes that infested those hills squirmed away through the grass, and there were lizards about.

High on one of the precipices a large heron of mature appearance was standing on a ledge, apparently attending to some domestic business in a nest. My two askaris were greatly stimulated by its presence. It would make an excellent dinner, they said, and seizing their rifles they prepared to shoot it. One of them, an old man with prominent ears, took the precaution of pushing a stick down the barrel first, to clean it: to nobody's surprise it stuck there, and sitting himself down beneath a bush he pulled and tugged and strained at it, wheezing and muttering hoarsely. Sometimes he held the butt between his knees and dragged at the stick with his teeth; sometimes his friend heaved at it; sometimes I did; sometimes he banged the barrel against a rock in an ill-advised effort to clear it by percussion: but it was all no good, and in the end we left him there, still muttering, and advanced through the grass without him. The second askari crept towards the heron with exaggerated caution, like a cat in a Disney cartoon, his rifle at his shoulder as he moved; and since the bird was perfectly still, and the range short, and the target clearly silhouetted, and the air calm, and the place silent (but for the subdued scurrilities behind us, still issuing from beneath the bush), I thought the chances of success were high. Alas! like Mr. Winkle, the askari had forgotten to load; and when, with a pitiful little click, he pulled the trigger, the heron looked lazily down from its height, shrugged its white shoulders patronizingly, joggled and steadied itself on its ledge, and flew heavily off to the cliff-top.

'Are there jinn in this place?' I inquired tactfully. The askari, who seemed to have forgotten the incident instantaneously, so bird-like were their little minds, shook their heads. Jinn, they said, haunted another pool, farther east: no, this pool was notorious for a large serpent which inhabited its innermost niches, and which from time to time emerged to assault the cattle of the Qara tribespeople. The hillmen, they said, did not like to frequent such places as this. What with the big snake, and the leopards supposed to live thereabouts, and the spirits of the dead who haunted the running waters, there was much to be said for keeping well away. A good thing, too, the askaris seemed to imply, for the Qara were barbarians anyway and would cut your throat for a dollar (and indeed, though seldom homicidal they did seem to be a troublesome, fractious kind of people).

On another occasion I drove east, in the company of an English Arabist living in Dhufar; past the tomb of the gigantic divine, past the Sultan's bewitching gardens, until we reached the village of Taqa, dominated by a strong surly fort upon a hill. Beyond this, down the coast, we could see the ruins of ancient Murbat, the pre-eminent frankincense mart, once a fine fortified port through which this country's aromatic products were exported, and goods of many gorgeous kinds passed on their way to the markets of northern and western Arabia. The Sabeans who built this city, which probably had its hey-day in the first century before Christ, then controlled most of the southern Arabian shore, from Aden to Dhufar: great traders and navigators, who settled their colonies and conducted their commerce as far north as Syria and Mesopotamia. Twenty centuries ago there was a well-frequented overland route from this city upon the Indian Ocean to the Nabatean stronghold of Petra, cut in the rocks of the Edom mountains a thousand miles to the north.

Taqa was a poor, pale substitute for that great seaport (monkeys and spices, Chinese silks, ivory, ostrich feathers,

Indian sword-blades, pearls from the Gulf) but it was the seat of a wali, local representative of the Sultan. Dhufar was governed as a Royal domain: the central government at Muscat, with its British Foreign Minister, had no authority there, and the walis were responsible directly to the ruler. We planned to leave the coast at Taqa and strike into the mountains, so we stopped there to pay our respects; and were briskly ushered into the small, clean mud-brick house in which the wali maintained his headquarters. He was a dignified, emaciated man with a Lee-Enfield rifle and a wrist-watch, and he led us up a narrow staircase to the roof. It was shaded by palm-fronds and lined with carpets. There we removed our shoes and sat down, the wali, the Arabist and I, and many courteous local dignitaries, sitting easily on the floor with their legs crossed, the hafts of their daggers glittering, the muzzles of their rifles pointing through the palm-fronds to the sky. Two big black man, soldiers of the Dhufar Force, knelt with their feet tucked beneath their bodies, in an attitude of graceful respect such as one sees portrayed in Egyptian tombs and temples. My neighbour, a young sheikh with an amiable hatchet face, drew his dagger to show me the quality of its Omani workmanship. The wali spread his skirts about him grandly and placed one horny hand upon his knee. We drank ginger tea.

'And did you see the new aeroplanes?' we asked politely.

'By Allah! We heard them scream, but did not see them. Tell us, how fast can they fly?'

'From here to Bahrain in ten minutes,' said my companion, a little wildly. 'To Aden in half an hour. From here to Jiddah and back again in an hour.'

'And what fuel do they use?'

'Kerosene. Have you got any kerosene?'

'Certainly we have.'

'Why don't you make yourselves an aeroplane, then? What use is firewood without a fire?'

The wali seemed a little puzzled by this observation, but

after some thought concluded it to be a joke, and laughed a
creaking laugh: soon, after an awkward fingering of their
robes, the dignitaries and the soldiers laughed too; and even
the coffee-pourer, parading about the room with a theatrical,
circus-like manipulation of his pot, pouring tea into cups with
conjurer's *panache*—even this enthusiast, intent upon his
pageantry, managed a distant smile.

During this muffled hilarity the Arabist, sitting there loosely
like an Arab himself, whispered to me: 'Your next-door neighbour but one is the Sultan's father-in-law!' I looked around,
across the hatchet-faced man, to a benign barefooted elder with
a tumbled turban, who was allowing himself a restrained but
pleasurable chuckle. The Sultan, Said bin Taimur, scion of the
Al bu Said dynasty, had married a Bedouin girl who lived in
honoured purdah in the palace at Salala and had borne him a
single son. Around every Oriental monarch there hangs an
agreeable suggestion of silky harems and discreet excesses, but
by all accounts the Sultan was a man of continence: and his
father-in-law had a reassuring country respectability about
him, redolent of prize-givings and parish committees.

Sages and urchins, indiscriminately mixed, said good-bye to
us as we took our leave of the wali and drove away from Taqa
towards the hills. A little way outside the village we found the
track blocked with big stones; the Qara people, it was explained to me, sometimes did things like that for no particular
reason, further evidence of a certain orneriness to their character. We cleared the way and were soon climbing out of the
plain. At that time of the year the seaward slopes of the
mountains were a dry rocky green, like Palestine, the scrubby
trees growing doggedly upon them. A few wild olives grew
there, intensifying the Mediterranean effect, and a fresh breeze
blew in from the sea, tangy with salt. Our track wound cir-
cuitously up the hill among crags, sometimes blocked by herds
of startled cattle, masterless and uncontrollable, and very soon
we had left the soft opulence of the plain behind us. The deeper
we penetrated into these Qara foot-hills, the more lifeless and

unearthly the country seemed. No tribespeople were to be seen, no serpent-ridden pools, and there was neither animation nor geniality to the landscape. It was like an empty Lebanon. Suddenly, however, the track turned a corner and there before me was one of the most extraordinary sights I have ever seen. Blocking the narrow valley in front of us stood the dramatic abyss of Dahaq, one of the wonders of Arabia, from which (according to some theorists) Ptolemy's city of Abyssapolis took its fascinating name.

The thing reminded me at once of Boulder or Grand Coulee, both in size and conception. At this point a stream called the Wadi Darbat, running down from the hills above, suddenly split into a number of rivulets and plunged over the precipice of Dahaq, 500 feet deep. The valley was narrow, both above and below the precipice, and the hills rose cruelly beside it on either side; but the cliff itself stood like some symbol of transition between life and death, or at least (I thought, for the simile had a morbid ring to it) between youth and age. At its foot the water splashed into a wadi that was lifeless and stony, softened only by a few trees and scattered shining pools; but above the cliff, squeezed between the hills, the valley of the Wadi Darbat was suddenly and breathtakingly fertile. There were fields of cotton and chilli, lavish palm trees, small neat clusters of hive-shaped huts; a little maze of fresh streams ran through the fields before leaping over the precipice and bounding to the rocks below; herds of cattle and goats grazed mildly, with none of that scrambling anarchy that had delayed our passage into the hills. This little Shangri-La stood poised on the brink of the big gloomy precipice, and its cultivated fields ran to the very edge and bulged over the cliff-face dangerously. Dahaq looked exactly like some great disused dam, pride of a distant century, whose reservoir had been blocked by generations of silt and left to become a garden.

Even then relatively few Europeans had visited this place, easily accessible though it was from Salala and the sea. The English explorers Mabel and Theodore Bent had been the first

to set eyes on Dahaq, in the 1890s; the next had been Bertram
Thomas, nearly forty years later. Since then the R.A.F. had
established its landing ground, and both airmen and oilmen
had come to know Dhufar; but so circumscribed had they
generally been by restrictions of one sort and another that not
many of them had made the journey. The valley still had some
of the indefinable allure of the little-known. We took off our
shoes and socks and rolled up our trousers and waded through
the streams and marshy banks that surrounded the settlement.
There was a dry route, but it zigzagged through the bog like the
track to some fenland hiding-place, and we preferred to take a
short cut. 'Look out for snakes!' said the askaris. 'Very bad
here!' But we emerged unbitten, and on the hard ground
beyond the marshes a few friendly villagers, having watched
our soggy progress with amusement, waited to meet us. They
were all negroes, in long robes and coloured turbans,
presumably descended from slaves freed from bondage on the
coast. One or two young women, unveiled and pretty, greeted
us with composure and murmured a few words of Arabic welcome; the women of freed slave families were the happiest in
Dhufar, for if their social status was no more than modest, their
liberty of action was complete. So black and raw-boned were
all these people, with their domed grass houses behind them,
the goats playing all around, the bright green of the crops and
the wind rustling through the trees, that for a moment Dahaq,
so near the southern coast of Arabia, felt like the heart of
Africa.

In single file, as if on safari, we walked through the well-
tended fields to the place where, with a disconcerting abrupt-
ness, the ground fell away. It recalled to me the famous precipice called El Capitan, in the Yosemite Valley, the top of which
I was once advised to approach on my stomach, to avoid
vertigo. Thomas, indeed, when he came to Dahaq in 1929, *did*
crawl to the edge of the abyss. We walked: but it was an uneasy
feeling to find a perfectly respectable field, neatly furrowed and
planted, suddenly ending in nothing at all. The cliff below

looked grim and uncompromising. A good rock climber could
have mastered it, but for ordinary people the only way was a
little winding track which cautiously ascended the western
flank. I was assured that camels sometimes used this steep
ladder to heaven.

We turned to leave, and the headman of the village, looking
about him hastily, grabbed a nearby goat in his two arms and
offered it to us as a farewell gift. When we refused it, thanking
him gratefully, he placed it on the ground again with an air of
unutterable disappointment. The bystanders, too, looked as if
they had experienced some severe personal loss. The women
shook their heads sadly, and even the goat, I thought, seemed a
little crestfallen. Seizing his moment competently, an old man
clutched my arm and said in a mournful voice:

'That there is a very sad tree. A tree of bitter memory!'

We looked at it, and asked him why. He told us that not long
before a young boy of the tribe had climbed on to its precarious
branches and had fallen headlong—*headlong*, repeated the old
man dramatically—to the ground below. He pointed to the
stony ground beneath it, where indeed I thought I detected
traces of blood.

'And what happened to the poor child?' asked the Arabist
tenderly.

'He broke his ankle.'

It was a melancholy moment. When we distributed pieces of
chocolate among them, though, everybody cheered up; and a
number of the more enthusiastic villagers guided us through
the little delta and pointed the way to a second wonder of the
Wadi Darbat. We proceeded up the valley, crossed a ridge,
meandered through a wide green water-meadow, and found
ourselves on the banks of a quiet placid lagoon, for all the world
like some small unfrequented lake in the English shires, fished
by railwaymen in the long summer evenings. Here none of the
Arabian symbols intruded—no camels, tents, plotting sheikhs,
veiled women, Cadillacs, battle-cries or oil rigs—and we sat
down miraculously among reeds and rushes and thick bushy

trees. Moorhens, of a kind, ruffled the surface of this lake; soft green grass ran down to the water's edge; 'better than the Backs', said my companion, 'not so many undergraduates.'

Nevertheless, though it was a place of overpowering peace and charm, and the askaris put their rifles down and tickled their toes with their canes, and I paddled my feet in the water and picked a few dainty flowers—nevertheless we were not alone. In the hillside above the lake we could see a warren and a complexity of caves and crannies, like the colony of some giant species of coney, or the cells of a multitude of Indian hermits. Rush mats covered some of their entrances, and outside others were rickety palm-frond structures. These were the homes of Qara mountaineers, half-way between the plains and the grazing grounds on the summit downs. A number of tribesmen stood beside their caves to watch us, and later several approached us with a diffident but reasonably agreeable welcome. Their long shaggy hair was held in place by leather thongs wound round the forehead, giving them, for some reason or other, an implausibly blue-stockinged appearance. Dark robes were slung around their middles and sometimes thrown over one shoulder, and stuck in a belt around the waist was almost invariably a dagger. Indigo streaked their faces (practically obliterating them sometimes); old rifles or sticks were in their hands; they talked to each other in a harsh and unidentifiable tongue, and seemed to understand only a word or two of Arabic. But, rough and illiterate though they were, and aboriginal in their bearing, their faces were sometimes of exceptional beauty and refinement. Some of the young men, with their delicate well-moulded features, offered profiles of a classic perfection; and they stood around to stare at us with a lovely open-air, natural grace. Do not think, though, that they were exemplars of that noble savage so dear to the eighteenth century. They were handsome enough, but rather wizened, small and stunted; and I am told they could be very mean.

There were four principal tribal groups of such people in

Dhufar. Each group spoke a different language, unwritten, and not understood by any of the others. 'It is believed by many Egyptologists', one of the old Luxor dragomen used to say with a scholarly air, 'that the origin of the Egyptians is not exactly known.' The same might be said of the Qara mountain people. Who they were, and where they came from, no one quite knew. They had peculiar *mores* of their own, with obscure rituals, taboos and prejudices. It was, for instance, forbidden for a woman to touch the udders of a cow, considered to be infinitely higher in the female scale of things. Indeed, in their respect for their cattle they seemed to have something in common with the Dinka tribesmen of the Sudan, whose sole lives, material and spiritual, revolved around their cows. Other, more definite African affinities had persuaded some anthropologists that the Qara people were Hamitic rather than Semitic, and there were said to be resemblances to the Fuzzy-Wuzzy people of the Red Sea coast of Africa. They might well be related; but the Qara tribes were probably survivors of the original inhabitants of southern Arabia, who lived in those parts before the Arab tribes swirled down from the desert.

Whatever they were, they were strange people to meet. On our way back to the plain we encountered a number of them, standing silently beside the track or throwing stones at their herds to move them out of the way. Later we saw two shaggy tribesmen saying their prayers. They were nominally Moslems, observing (for example) the Islamic fast of Ramadan, but their theological principles seemed to be a trifle hazy: whenever I saw any of them praying during my stay in Dhufar, they were turned not towards Mecca, but towards the sun. Once an old woman stopped us to offer us a pigeon. We had no money, and told her so: but she pressed it on us anyway, and we ate it for supper: for pigeons, like other birds, hyenas, foxes, chickens and all kinds of eggs, were taboo to these opinionated people.

Thus, in exploring this enthralling country, the days passed. Soon good news began to arrive from the interior, where the campaign had been launched according to schedule. Most of the news came over the R.A.F. wireless system; the efficient young flying officer who commanded the station (the only officer there) prefaced each brusque operation message with the courtly phrase 'Your Highness; After Compliments', and sent it down to the palace. Other items of information seemed to arrive from over the mountains by the inexplicable medium of the Arab grape vine.

All appeared to be going well. The Field Force had advanced from Fahud to Nizwa, in conditions of great secrecy. At a village improbably called Firq a single shot was fired at the soldiery, missing them all; but when the force encamped outside the capital, it appeared, most of the opposition had instinctively evaporated. We did not yet know what had become of the Imam or his brother; nor how determined were his supporters deeper in the mountains; nor what was happening to the Batinah Force. The Imam's representative in Cairo had announced extravagantly that general mobilization had been ordered in the Imamate; and in a broadcast to his fellow subjects he had said that God and the Prophet commanded them to 'stand like a solid steel barrier against the forces of imperialism'. Still, the first auguries were favourable, and messages of tentative congratulations began to reach the Sultan. The King of Libya, whose population included a substantial number of Ibhadis, announced that his army would *not* march to the aid of the Imam: a promise which, though obliging, did not seem to take any great weight off anybody's mind. A communiqué issued by the Sultan's Foreign Minister in Muscat revealed that the war had begun, and spoke of the Sultan's armies marching upon 'the traitor Ghaleb'. The British authorities assured the world that it was a purely internal affair. All in all, things seemed to be satisfactory; and the Sultan prepared to leave on his long victory march, telling scarcely a soul in Salala where he was going.

I packed my bags and sharpened my pencils: and promptly at the appointed time, in the hot sun of the early afternoon, a bright yellow American sports car arrived outside my hut at the landing ground. Its driver, a big barefooted negro, slung my bags easily into the back seat; and so determined a driver was this man, and with such abandon did we fly through the streets of Salala, with such a raising of dust and skidding of tyres and terrifying of pedestrians, that in a matter of moments we were at the entrance to the palace, and the big slaves opened the gates for me, and a little crowd of townsmen and tribespeople, leaning on their sticks and firearms, looked on dully like provincials in a football queue.

3

The convoy—exhilarating start—in the hills—the frankincense tree—Wadi Duka—across the gravel desert —swift progress—the dump—more good news—the Empty Quarter—Fahud

'I see,' said the Sultan, as we walked together down the hall, followed by a small train of picturesque officials. 'Then I think you will find this map, produced by Mr. Bertram Thomas, a useful travelling companion. He was my father's Wazir, you know: a very interesting man.'

Outside the door there stood a stubby, powerful American truck, piled high with baggage, and beside it the Sultan stopped and unfolded the map. I stood over him, taller by a foot or more, and examined his face while he pointed out the route to me. He was only 44, but the voluminous dignity of his robes, his stately bearing, his heavy turban and his luxuriant beard all combined to make him look much older. His eyes were large, dark, long-lashed and very serious. His mouth, though kindly and humorous, looked to me capable of an occasional sneer, and often seemed to act independently of the rest of his features. It was an antique, melancholy face, such as you might see in old pictures from the East; tempered, indeed, by education and by long years of association with westerners;

but still, I thought, as profoundly enigmatical as the Pyramids. When the Sultan looked up at me from the map, his eyes were full of eager intelligence; later I was to see them immensely proud and overbearing; and I was to learn the infinite adaptability of the phrase 'I see', as used by the Sultan of Muscat and Oman.

The driver of the truck stood trembling beside the door, and the Sultan clambered in athletically. I watched him hitch up his robe, adjust his sword, arrange his papers and settle himself in the front seat. With deliberate care he put on a pair of sunglasses, and the driver jumped in and started the engine.

'Now, Mr. Morris,' said the Sultan. 'If you are ready I think we might start. It will be an interesting journey, I think. I hope you will be comfortable, and if there is anything at all you want, please let my people know.'

I bowed; he smiled; the retainers in the hall clanked their rifles; and I walked from the inner courtyard into the big yard outside. There stood our convoy, ready for the journey. There were six more American trucks, all identical, piled almost to overturning with stores and bags. Each carried its complement of strong negro slaves, wearing blue jerseys like sailors of the Royal Navy or skippers of *Skylarks* at far-away piers. In one vehicle five small goats, doomed but stoical, stood with their heads just showing above the side, their ears waggling vigorously. In the front seats of others a strange assortment of dignitaries was sitting, and I had a smudged glimpse of beards, turbans, rifles, daggers and bright eyes as I hastened across the yard. The convoy was already infused with a sense of high excitement, and there was a champagne feeling in the air. The Sultan was evidently a man of punctuality. The engines were already racing, the slaves were clinging precariously to the mountains of stores. 'Here, Sahib! This way!' said two smiling negroes, running across the yard to meet me. 'Your bags are in. Welcome!' And practically frog-marching me across the courtyard they guided me to my truck, its door already open, its driver grinning at me from inside. I jumped into my seat;

the slaves climbed agilely up behind; and at that very instant there was a loud insistent blare of the Sultan's horn. The trucks leapt away like dogs from the leash, manœuvring for position. Exhaust smoke billowed about the palace. We were off! At breakneck speed our convoy drove out of the yard. The slaves struck up a loud unison fatha, invoking blessings on our mission. The household retainers lining the several courtyards bowed low and very humbly, and some of the men prostrated themselves. The keepers of the portals swung open the gates with a crash. The bystanders waved their sticks and shouted loyal greetings. The slave-girls of Salala, after preliminary reconnaissances, ran giggling into their houses with flying draperies. With a tremendous roaring of engines we rushed through the town and into the plain, and even the old camels, labouring around their wells, looked up for a bleary moment to watch us pass.

First went a truck flying the red flag of Muscat. Beside its driver sat our Bedouin guide, a small withered man with an avaricious look about him. Next rode the Sultan, his big turban bobbing up and down with the bumps of the track. In the third truck sat an elderly functionary with a long white beard; in the fourth were two splendid desert sheikhs, crowded together over the gear-box, with their rifles protruding from the window; in the fifth was a very old qadi of saintly bearing; and the rest of us followed behind, at tremendous speed, jolting wildly over the plain like raiders hot on the heels of an enemy. The flag flapped bravely. The big slaves laughed at each other and clutched their weapons. The little goats huddled together for company. It was a gloriously exhilarating start.

'Where are we going?' inquired my driver, a friendly man from the Hadramaut.

'D'you mean to say you don't know?'

'We none of us know. We never do, when we go on a journey with the Sultan. Are we going into the desert?'

'We are going *across* the desert,' I said, 'but more than that I

41

suppose I'd better not tell you. Have you been this way before?'

'Into the mountains, not beyond. I hope we travel very far. I want to see all the cities of this country, and all the mountains. And the other sea, too! You see' (he added earnestly) 'I have a very young wife at Aden, she is only aged sixteen, and I think it is good for her to hear of all these different places. So we're going across the desert, are we? Good! Very good!'

From beneath his seat he pulled out a chunk of dry bread, and tearing it in half he handed one part to me. We sat there munching cheerfully, he singing a tuneless song, I thinking about our journey, the two of us bouncing jerkily but rhythmically, side by side.

'The Sultan travels very fast,' said the driver, 'but have no fear. I am a very good mechanic, and God will protect us. This is a strong truck, don't be afraid, we shall survive, God willing!'

'God willing!' I echoed with feeling, for it seemed to me that judging by the pace we were travelling, the wild gusto of the drivers, the roughness of the road, and the general feeling of boisterous *bonhomie*, the divine goodwill would certainly be needed.

We swept across the plain of Jurbaib grandly; the Arabs standing beside the track were so struck by our majestic manner that they did not even ask us for a lift (they usually seemed unaccountably eager to go just wherever the passing truck was going). Soon we were climbing into the hills, through that empty scrubby country I had seen before, with a few stunted trees growing among the stones. We were following the oilmen's route through the mountains, through the Kismim pass and up a dry watercourse called the Wadi Duka. The track was therefore good. It was also very steep, and as we raced up it, swinging daringly around its corners and beside its many precipices, I could hear the slaves behind me gasping and murmuring to themselves. I imagine that (like me) they were assuring Allah of their trust in his benevolence.

Anyway, this tortuous and tempestuous progress, rather like one of the more abandoned British hill-climbing contests, did not last long; for after a few hours we emerged upon the delightful upland downs of the Qara mountains. It felt like England without its churches, or Kentucky without its white palings. The grass was not quite so inviting, perhaps, but was a heavenly yellowish-green all the same. Groves of thick trees studded the landscape, and the hills rolled away into the distance gentle and serene, for all the world like some unspoilt English downland. Housman would have felt at home here; Hardy, if he had strayed to Dhufar, might well have expected some pungent Dorset countryman to appear over the next ridge; and Borrow could have tackled the Flaming Tinman without much incongruity in one of these secluded dingles. There were herds of fat cattle about, rather like Jerseys, which looked as though they might well be slowly wandering, as the afternoon drew on, towards some soft-scented English farmyard. Clumps of a rhododendron-like bush brightened the fresh meadows, and I asked the driver to stop while I jumped hurriedly out of the truck to pick some blossoms. The driver behind us leant out to wave as he roared bravely past, and the slaves on the back of his truck shouted and laughed at the slaves on the back of ours.

'What do you want them for?' asked the driver when I returned with the flowers. 'Are they good for diseases?'

'I don't think so. I just thought they looked nice.'

'So they do, so they do. But the Qara people eat them, for the stomach.'

'Are you *sure*?'

'Quite sure. The Qara people know everything about the flowers and things. They're very strange people, like the animals. By Allah! They are very like the animals!'

As if to bear him out, we saw at that moment three strange fuzzy tribesmen standing on a bank beside the road. My driver, laughing conspiratorially at me, shouted them a ribald greeting. Two of them, with long, beautiful faces, did not respond, but simply stood there stiffly, like childish elocutionists awaiting their turn to perform; the third, a younger man, ventured to wave his short stick at us, and then, seeing that his companions remained impassive, lowered it again shamefacedly as if guilty of some desperate solecism. When we had passed I leant out of the window to look back at them. There they were still, three straight, shy figures, holding their sticks, watching our progress fixedly. If they were a little suspicious, it was understandable. They lived a precarious life in the mountains. Feuds between families and clans were common: and people living in one valley, speaking their own language, had little intercourse with the people living in the next, speaking *theirs*—on the contrary, the two were very likely hereditary enemies, and would shoot at each other when feasible, or hurl in the general direction of their neighbours the heavy throwing-sticks (less scientific than boomerangs) with which they were sometimes quaintly armed.

Sometimes we saw their caves in the hillsides. I tried to imagine it up here in the monsoon, with the damp and the fog swirling in and out of their homes, and remembered the wet weather in the high Nepalese Himalaya, in which the mist, the alpine flowers, the looming figures of Sherpa hillmen, the rocks and the dripping trees all seemed to be mixed up in one dismal recollection. No wonder, I thought, that for all their fat cattle and delectable grazing grounds the Qara tribesmen had a strained and begrudging air to them.

We left their country as quickly as we had entered it. The capricious monsoon, having picked Dhufar as its only call in the Arabian Peninsula, does not touch the northern side of the Qara mountains. At the crest of the hills the country therefore changes abruptly, exactly as, in the north-west corner of the United States, the ridge of the Cascade Mountains divides the coastal lumber country from the orchards and wheatfields of inland Washington. Crossing the Cascades you often pass from drizzle to dazzling sunshine: crossing the Qara mountains you move, in a manner almost allegorical, like the cliff at Dahaq, from meadows to desolation. One minute the trees and the cows are with you; the next the country is dry and harsh, and littered with boulders and grim pyramidical hillocks. We crossed this line in the afternoon to see almost at once, in a plateau on the gradual northern slopes, a herd of gazelle. The truck in front of us stopped instantly; the two sheikhs leapt out with their new Lee-Enfield rifles; they stalked their prey, raised their rifles, missed, roared with laughter, and ran back to the truck: and on we went again in high spirits, racing after the red flag and the Sultan as they disappeared into the distance. The plain and the mountains were behind us. This was the country of gazelle and riflemen and Bedouin gaiety.

Here and there were small groves of a queer, twisted sort of tree, looking about a million years old, and graced only with a modicum of obstinate life: the frankincense tree. It only seemed to grow on this dry side of the mountains, its nature apparently being affined to things mournful and austere. In the great days of the frankincense industry the rulers of the coast, who enjoyed a monopoly of it, would send their criminals in chained gangs to gather the sap. Now, in a secular world, incense was in less demand and the work was done by private enterprise. The women of the tribes visited the groves from time to time, made incisions in the tree-trunks, and returned some days later to gather the oozing sap. Most of the incense left Dhufar by slow-sailing dhows: no steamships ever called at Salala (when the Sultan wanted a speedy sea passage somewhere he generally arranged a passage on a passing tanker) and the small freighters that put in at the oil camp were far too concerned with girders and machinery to bother with such spiced eccentric cargoes. Once the incense went chiefly west and north, to Egypt and Syria—indeed, in the alley-way outside the Church of the Holy Sepulchre in Jerusalem I had myself been offered incense which had come, so I was assured, from the southern coast of Arabia: but nowadays most of it went eastwards to the temples of India. It was queer to think, as we drove down the hills, that the excretion of those gloomy trees might play its part in the gilded rituals of Kandy or Benares.

We did not stop for a moment that afternoon, but drove out of the hills in the gathering dusk and up the bed of the Wadi Duka. There was nothing to see but a wide dry plain with a few trees in it. No animals crossed our path; no birds flew over us; we simply followed the track of the oil trucks, the dust flying away from us like the spray from a squadron of boats, until we saw in a distant fold in the plain the huts and machinery of the oil camp. The Sultan's truck stopped, and the others lined themselves up neatly at a decorous distance. In a trice the slaves were off and unpacking the bags at headlong speed. There were hoarse shouts, the clatter of tent poles, the banging of bags, the baying of goats. Before I had time to stretch my legs the tents were going up—one, on the fringe of the camp, for the Sultan; one for the elderly functionaries; one for the two sheikhs and their various followers; and one for me. Soon a fire was burning merrily, and dark shapes were bustling about it with pots and pans. There was the sound of pouring water, and the sizzle of fat. Away in the distance I could hear the faint chugging of the oil camp's generator: here, now that the trucks were silent, there were only the immemorial travellers' noises.

I walked away to pay my respects to the Sultan, whose small, plump but erect figure I could see standing statuesque outside his tent: but I was forestalled. All those journeying dignitaries were moving towards him in a ragged procession, carrying their rifles, and after bowing solemnly they formed a wide semicircle around his presence. My driver identified them for me. The elderly official was another wali from Dhufar, a senior representative of the Sultan in that province: he suggested to me an Arabian Polonius, for his manner was grand but indecisive and there was, I thought, something rather feeble about his face. The saintly old scholar was the qadi of Salala, at once jurist and cleric, a man of happy disposition, sprightly if decrepit. The two sheikhs, who looked to me like identical twins, were leaders of the Yal Wahiba tribe, a powerful group, famous for audacity and hospitality, which lived in the country to the east: a genuinely nomadic people, always on the move, whose only settled property was a village on the desert's edge where the paramount sheikh was said to spend his summers. There was a sickly-looking youth in a turban rather too big for him, who was pointed out to me as the son of some paramount chief or other, I forget which; and a number of cheerful ignorant Bedouin, all guns and smiles, who were followers of the Yal Wahiba sheikhs.

This was the company; and they all stood there silently around the Sultan. Sometimes the Sultan murmured something in a low voice, and the wali answered respectfully. Generally everybody stood mutely, wali, qadi, sheikhs, son of the paramount chief, followers, Sultan and all: until by some imperceptible or even telepathic gesture the Sultan dispersed the assembly. As they withdrew, I advanced.

'It was an interesting journey, don't you think?' said the Sultan. 'A little rough, perhaps. You know, I built the road over the mountains myself, for the benefit of the oil company. It is sometimes very steep.'

'We seem to have made very good time, Your Highness. How many miles do you suppose we've come?'

'I checked it on my speedometer. We began at 446. It now reads 559. That is—let me see—113 miles, I think. I like to travel fast. I hope you had a comfortable journey, nevertheless? My people are looking after you? You are not too tired?'

'If I *were* tired, sir,' I replied, 'I certainly wouldn't say so.'

'I see, Mr. Morris,' said the Sultan, with an enigmatic smile; and we parted. When I walked back to the camp again, I found that my bags had already been removed from the truck, my tent was erected, and a company of smiling attendants was awaiting my pleasure.

'All ready!' said the brawny slave who had apparently undertaken to pay particular attention to me. 'Come and see!'

There was my camp bed, skilfully assembled, with two blankets arranged upon it in a complex and (it later proved) almost impenetrable system. A handsome carpet was on the ground. A packet of biscuits and my typewriter were placed invitingly in the middle of it, as if one would be perfectly useless without the other; my old khaki greatcoat hung from the tentpole; and on a fine burnished tray beside the door was a blue china teapot and a cup and saucer.

'Tea!' announced the slave, with a noble smile; and the retainers who had helped in the preparation of the tent bowed respectfully to me and withdrew. The Arab always knows when to leave you alone; and I drank my tea in peaceful and welcome solitude. (Throughout the journey my companions were especially solicitous in helping me to work, demanding from each other an unearthly silence if ever I was writing in their neighbourhood. I could not help contrasting the situation a century before, when the indomitable Richard Burton, travelling in Arabia in very different circumstances, could only manage to keep his notes by questioning the snobbish Arabs on their genealogy and pretending to jot down details of their ineffably boring antecedents—all the time recording the facts and impressions of his travels.)

It used to be the custom of the Arab traveller to make his first day's journey a short one, so that if he had forgotten anything crucial he could always go back and get it. The Sultan had decided to observe this tradition, at once (unlike so many other hoary customs) time-honoured and sensible. We had not really begun our crossing into Oman, but had merely driven to the end of the track, ready to launch ourselves into the desert the next morning. On this first day we had travelled northward. Tomorrow we would turn east. I spent an hour or two that evening tracing our route upon the map and meditating upon our fortunes; and when the slave arrived with a big plate of goats' kidneys, with trimmings of rice and spices, puri (wheat wafers cooked in ghee), more tea and a bowl of tinned fruit, I ate it all gratefully, turned down my hurricane lamp, and slept.

The Sultan's lamp burned late, and the glow of the big camp-fire only died away in the small hours of the morning.

Soon after dawn we moved into the Jaddat al Harasis, and raced for three solid days, with scarcely a halt except at night time, across that great gravel waste. It had only been crossed by Europeans once or twice before, and then by very different routes; and no motor vehicle had ever travelled across it from one side to the other. During the first morning of our journey wheel tracks and traces of bivouacs showed that oil prospectors had passed that way; and long after we had left Wadi Duka we saw in the distance, like a token of some self-denying faith, a tall steel derrick implanted in the desert and served by a dedicated group of acolytes. After that there was no life at all but a small flock of embarrassed birds, who flew hastily away as if they had been caught eating jam in the pantry, and one solitary emaciated camel. The Jaddat al Harasis was a wide stony plain, almost waterless, lying between the coastal mountains and the Empty Quarter. A few dry wadi beds crossed it. Some withered thorny plants grew in it. Sometimes the flat gravel of its surface degenerated into a mess of big stones and boulders, tumbled all together like a monstrous pebble beach, and singularly uncomfortable to traverse. For 200 miles or more we saw no signs of humanity, but in fact a poor tribe of primitive nomads, apparently non-Arab and akin to the Qara hill-men, wandered hopelessly in these wastes, speaking its own language: the existence of these people, the Harasis, was unsuspected until Bertram Thomas, 'a very interesting man', discovered their presence in 1931.

Our progress was generally extremely fast, but more exhausting than it was hazardous. Widely dispersed across the plain, the seven trucks rocked and jolted riotously over the gravel, the slaves hanging on for dear life, the flag streaming, the speckled goats (already reduced in numbers) bumping beside the cooking pans with their eyes closed. Nobody waited for anyone else, but merely dashed inexorably onwards as fast as possible, only keeping an eye on the tracks made by the leading truck, in which that hard-eyed Bedouin guide supposedly knew where he was going. No obstacle was too much for us. If it was a wide wadi bed clogged with boulders, we drove straight into it, flat out, clenching our nerves and praying, and holding hard to our seats during the nightmare switchback ride across it. If it was a huge soft sand-patch, we entered it similarly at top speed with a frenzied rotating motion of the steering wheel. This usually worked well, but if (as sometimes happened) we found ourselves stuck, and a grinding procession through the gears failed to free us, the slaves were off the baggage in a twinkling of an eye and pushing us from behind with chanting and grunting noises. Once, at such a moment, I looked around me to see scattered over the desert, almost to the horizon, all our seven trucks simultaneously stuck, each with its little train of black pushers heaving manfully at it from the rear; and when, one by one, the trucks were freed and shot suddenly forwards the slaves ran after them like steeple-chasers or dervishes and with desperate leaps regained their places among the impedimenta.

We did not stop to eat, or check our tyres, or lie in the shade beneath our trucks, as soldiers or lorry-drivers do: but at midday the convoy halted for prayers. Then the whole company, except perhaps a few profane and impenitent servants, scattered modestly over the desert and performed first their ablutions and then their devotions: the negroes in their blue sweaters; the Bedouin, placing their rifles on the ground beside them, in their fine flowing robes; the qadi, with an audible creaking of his bones; the Sultan, now dressed in a fawn-coloured robe for travelling. It was a moving sight, I thought, to see them speckling the desert around us, blue and black and brown and white, prostrating themselves in the sunshine with the supple and graceful motions that Islam demands of its faithful: and when the Sultan's horn sounded in the distance, it was fun to see them come hurrying back again to jump in the trucks, in such a wild and often impeding variety of costumes;

the Yal Wahiba sheikhs always last of all, moving with a lively jerky trot, like magnificent big birds. Sometimes, during these brief halts, the servants brought me biscuits and even tea, swiftly prepared. Once a man arrived with two fine fossilized shells, picked up by the Sultan and sent over with his compliments. ('I am very interested in these things, you see, because of the possibilities of mineral wealth in this country. Several people have looked at parts of it, from a geological point of view, you see, but we have never had it all properly surveyed. I am especially interested in such matters.')

In such swift and exhilarating activity the hours passed quickly. Each day we started early and ended our journey at sunset. There were a few unintentional halts. Once a goat fell off and had to be picked up, none the worse, by the truck behind; sometimes there were punctures, expeditiously repaired by the slaves; once or twice a piece of baggage was jolted so violently that it burst or sagged or slipped its moorings, or a goatskin water-bag, flapping against the back of a truck, had to be more securely fastened. In general, though, our progress was unrelenting; and since everything, from dawn to dark, was done at the double to the strictest possible timetable, by the end of the day the company was noticeably fatigued.

Each evening, nevertheless, the Sultan would hold his subdued *majlis*, standing serene among the decorative garland of his Arabs. Once a small deputation of the Yal Wahiba Bedouin formed up to make a complaint. The baggage on top of which they were travelling was piled so high and so perilously, they said, and the speed of everything was so extreme, that they were afraid they were going to fall off, like the goat. By God! said they, it was extremely dangerous to travel like that! The Sultan greeted them with a wry amused detachment. What did they expect him to do about it? Jettison the baggage? Abandon the journey? They would just have to hold on, wouldn't they? The Bedouin laughed a little sheepishly, and returned to the small tight circle in which, squatting on the ground with their rifles upright beside them, they passed the time in desultory chatter. They had no jobs to do, but sat there talking and joking until the negro cooks, banging their huge bowls, rolling out their puris, blowing at their big wood fires, produced something to eat.

Sometimes I joined the Bedouin in their circle, which, although of a certain geometrical primness of form, was an agreeable and humorous assembly. Sometimes the wali joined us, and sat on his haunches ponderously. Once, I remember, the Bedouin questioned him about events in the interior, and he answered with a true courtier's facility.

'The Imam, wali,' said a young Bedu, 'what has become of him?'

'There is no Imam.'

'No Imam? What has become of him? Is he dead? Where is he?'

'There is no Imam,' said the wali. 'Only the Sultan, on whom God's blessing fall!'

'Thanks be to God!' said the Bedouin properly; and the old qadi, tottering by, paused to conclude the exchange with a trembling but sonorous echo.

Our starts each morning were performed with dramatic intensity. The nights on that high plateau were bitterly cold. I slept in my clothes, having pierced that baffling arrangement of blankets (repeated scrupulously each night by the conscientious bondsmen) and covered my bed with my jacket, my greatcoat and any odd fabrics or materials I found in the bottom of my bag. Nevertheless I woke shivering each morning long before dawn, only to find that the camp was already astir in the darkness. There would be a soft padding of feet outside my tent, the clink of the pans, a hum of murmuring voices. The first crackle of the fire followed. As the sun came up, so my breakfast arrived—tea and biscuits, followed by goats' meat tasting strongly of the fat it was cooked in: and almost simultaneously, with a crash, the camp was struck. Like locusts the

slaves fell upon the tents, ten men to each one. Out with the
tent pegs! Down with the pole! Wind the ropes up, roll the
canvas! The poor Bedouin, already sitting in their formal
circle, found their tent whisked away from over their heads.
The qadi stumbled out still doing up his turban, like a housewife in pins giving her sleepy instructions to the milkman. I just
had time to take my kidneys outside before my own tent disappeared, my camp bed was folded and tied, my bag was packed,
and my binoculars, maps, notebooks and camera were whisked
away to the truck. A moment later the first engines were
revving and the goats were being hoisted aboard. The bags
were loaded and strapped; the slaves seized their rifles; and
when the sharp toot of the Sultan's horn sounded over the
morning air, hey presto! like magic we all swooped away.
'Whiz whiz! all done by steam!' said the Pasha to Kinglake,
trying to epitomize the English way of life; but nothing could
be more brilliantly machine-like than the Sultan's progress into
Oman.

He was obviously enjoying every moment of it. The
planning and control of our expedition was all his. He knew
our mileage exactly, our position, our water and fuel supplies,
our expected time of arrival, our average speed. In a canvas
bag lined with waterproof plastic, such as American women
sometimes pack with tinned soups and Kleenex at the super-
market, he carried his instruments—binoculars, thermometer,
altimeter, two prismatic compasses. His maps were carefully
annotated. His log was accurately kept. Never was there a
more thorough royal traveller.

A little too thorough, perhaps, for the Bedouin guide. One
evening I overheard the Sultan giving him what could only be,
by the tone of its delivery, a fairly effective reprimand; at the
end of which the guide, whose leadership that day had certainly
seemed a little erratic, slunk away like a dog abused.

'He has guided us very poorly today,' said the Sultan, turning to me. 'At one time this afternoon we were a long way off
our correct route. I had to tell him so. If he cannot guide us

properly there is no point in having him with us.'

The guide never quite seemed to recover from this incident (which did, after all, appear to show that his presence was not so essential as we all thought it to be); and I was later told that he had entered the Sultan's service by unorthodox means. He had been, it appeared, a famous carrier of illicit goods between the hinterland and the coast, a trade which gave him an exceptional knowledge of the country; and when he was eventually arrested the Sultan decided to make use of his criminal talents instead of throwing him into the customary dungeon. Poor man, he probably thought that evening that irons were awaiting him: but when I left Arabia he was still the Sultan's desert guide, and was still (like Scheherazade) managing to postpone his deserts.

One by one the goats paid their penalty, and our inanimate supplies also began to run low. But after three days of such hectic (and sometimes hilarious) travelling we saw on the distant horizon a smudged black blob. The guide must have thanked his God for new mercies, for this was a dump of stores deposited there for us, and vital to our continued progress. At the eastern end of the Jaddat al Harasis American oilmen were active, but we had now crossed the border from Dhufar into Oman—a border clearly defined by the Sultan—and here the concessionary company was British. The Fahud prospectors flew some of their supplies in, but shipped the rest through a village port on the southern coast called Dukam; and from the coast to the oil area they had stamped themselves a route across the desert. This we were now reaching, and on it we would turn north into the Oman hinterland. The Sultan had arranged that stocks of petrol and water should be left there for us; and as we approached we saw that sitting beside the big pile of cans, tanks and water containers was a disconsolate-looking sheikh of faded official bearing. He was one of the Sultan's representatives in Dukam and had been dumped there, like the oil cans, to await our arrival. We must have been visible for miles as we

roared across the desert towards him: but we were almost upon
him before he looked up with a violent start and began to
prepare himself with tuggings at his robes and rearrangements
of his fittings, for the royal visitation.

We halted with our usual screaming and skidding, and the
servants jumped off to do their business. The petrol tanks were
filled to overflowing (the fuel was provided by the oil company,
and it was improbable that the Sultan would ever get a bill for
it). The goatskin water-bags bulged again. All down the line of
the trucks, impeccably paraded, drivers brandished their dip-
sticks with florid gestures. I looked for the Sultan, but he had
walked far away from the trucks for a conference with the official from Dukam. There they were in the distance, two little
figures sitting cross-legged in the shade of a bloodless tree.
They sat facing one another, with a substantial gap separating
them, and the sun glinted on the silver handles of their daggers.
Once a slave, wearing what appeared to be a pleated tartan
skirt beneath his sweater, hurried across to them with coffee;
but generally the Sultan and his minion sat there alone in
earnest conversation. With their beards, their big turbans,
their antique cross-legged attitudes, and their manner of
scholarly calm, they looked like figures from a Persian minia-
ture: only the wine was lacking, in that ascetic Arab society.

The official had brought good news. Nizwa had capitulated
without a shot, and the Imam, finding his supporters reluctant
to make a fight of it, had climbed over the wall of his fort in the
middle of the night, swarmed down a rope, and ridden away
into the mountains on a donkey. His whereabouts were not yet
known. His brother Talib, after leading a tough resistance on
the seaward side of the mountains, had also vanished. The
Sultan's army had entered Nizwa and was now encamped in a
plain outside its walls. Our theatrical approach was still all
unknown, for nobody knew what fanatics still muttered in the
hills, nor whether the Imam was preparing a counter-attack:
but we could proceed inland with reasonable confidence, and
(it was thought) the sooner the Sultan appeared in the capitu-

lated capital, the better it would be.

We drove long after dark that night, and started at crack of dawn next day. The track was good and we sped merrily along it, raising clouds of dust, till the negroid faces of the retainers were coated with an eerie chalky film, masking everything but their big white eyes and their flashing teeth. I looked up once to see the huge horny feet of a slave hanging beside my ear: so rollicking, indeed, was our progress that I half expected to hear Bob Sawyer's voice from the roof above, or find his brandy bottle swaying outside my window. Soon we saw in the extreme distance a blue ridge of mountains; and our track—sometimes disintegrating into nebulous ruts, sometimes firm and well-defined—now led us between rolling sand-dunes of a splendid golden colour. Once I asked the driver to stop, and climbed laboriously, sinking in the soft sand, to the top of one of these dunes. To the north were the scurrying dust-trails of our convoy, fast receding, and beyond them the distant hills. But to the west all was emptiness. I was standing on the rim of the Empty Quarter, where the sand came up to the steppes. There was nothing much but desert between me and Mecca. The dunes stretched away lethargically, and I remembered with a shudder the English explorers who had launched themselves into that drab greedy wilderness with only their camels and wild Arabs for companionship. Away to the north-west there was a big white patch that looked like salt-flats—the notorious quicksands called the Umm as Samim, through which only the Duru Bedouin knew a safe way, and in which many poor Arabs had been engulfed with their animals. It was an uncomforting view. I turned around and slid down the sand-dune on my bottom, wishing I had a tea-tray; and in a moment we were rocketing northwards again, trying to catch up the Sultan.

Presently some small signs of fecundity began to appear in the plain. There were little plants with pink blossoms. A fly found its way into the cab of my truck. Here and there groves of brambly trees showed the presence of water, and out of one of them there flew a couple of brown birds. (In this area, I was told, somebody had recently shot a cheetah, at last confirming the zoologists' belief that this animal survived in a few corners of Arabia. There were lions in Iraq until 1935, and ostriches in the peninsula until thirty or forty years ago, and elephants at Aswan—if you believe the dragomen—in the last century: but in general the animal life of the Middle East lacks splendour or exoticism, and the pi-dog and the scavenging hawk are its unstimulating figure-heads.)

Then we reached humanity. The first strangers we had encountered for 400 miles (not counting the official from Dukam) were two scrawny figures, dressed in rags, who ran out of a wadi-bed to see us pass, and waved a timid reply to our greeting. Half an hour later we passed a huge oil lorry parked beside the track. A Land Rover approached, stopped, and turned around again to guide us: and long after dark we saw in front of us the few dim lights of Fahud. We had crossed the Jeddat al Harasis and were now, 600 miles from Salala, on the threshold of the mountains.

4

Interlude with oil rig

The Sultan established his camp outside the oil settlement, near a collection of palm-frond huts (called burastis) which housed those members of the local tribes lucky enough to have found jobs there. I prepared to sleep there too, but the oilmen invited me to spend the night with them; so happily throwing my bags into the back of a Land Rover, and telling my driver he could eat my share of the goats' kidneys, I drove away into the oil camp. Not far from Fahud a sizeable strip had been laid, and for many weeks a big British freighter aircraft had been making almost daily flights there, ferrying equipment from Bahrain; some of the things it carried were very large and unwieldy, and its manufacturers claimed that no operation of quite the same magnitude and character had ever been undertaken before. It was certainly remarkable to find, plumb in the middle of an almost unexplored territory, in a spot where (as it happened) there was no drinking water at all, a settlement so comfortably and even luxuriously appointed. The huts of Fahud were raised on blocks above the duty gravel, I forget why, so that my first impression was of an unusually well-appointed bathing-beach. Living in one of these huts, however, was more like living in a long-range airliner. Each was divided into four rooms (bedside lamps, rugs, white sheets), so neat and cosy that you almost expected the stewardess to bring you the morning paper, or the captain to begin one of those paralyzing attempts to put his passengers at ease. Each was extremely well air-conditioned. There were showers, using a brackish water available under the ground there, piping hot both day and night. Everything was spotless, and new, and sensible, and had a kind of aluminium flavour even when it was made of some quite different substance. All in all, much though I was enjoying the Sultan's journey, I bounced on my bed that night (to test the springs) with some degree of elation.

The mess was even better. It had, it was true, a certain beery, pin-up, Sunday-paperish tone, but the people were friendly and the menu was mouth-watering. Not only was there a very wide choice of dishes, but there seemed to be an endless supply of such things as beef-steaks and butter not commonly associated with trackless wildernesses. Nobody would go and work at a place like Fahud, they told me, *sans* women, *sans* pub, *sans* almost everything, unless they were assured of a few basic creature comforts. The Sultan would not allow spirits at Fahud, but large quantities of beer were brought in, and all kinds of advanced comestibles. Some of these provisions were flown there, some came by sea along the incense coast from Aden, to be unloaded at that remote Arabian cove at Dukam and conveyed along the fringes of the Rub al Khali. Silks, spices and monkeys had once made their way northward through Arabia: now it was beer.

We set off in convoy, in the bright cool sunshine of the early morning to visit the oil rig: a place of understandable interest to the Sultan, who stood to become a multi-millionaire because of it, and indeed to every loyal supporter of the pound sterling. The day for drilling to begin was now very near. The oilmen hoped that if all went well with the Sultan's affairs the rig would be fully at work by the middle of January, only a few last fittings now being necessary to complete it. I asked the Sultan if he was planning another visit to Fahud to turn the handle ceremonially and set the rig drilling.

'I do not think so,' he said. 'I once agreed to do that with the American oil company, in Dhufar, but when they had drilled to a depth of many thousand feet they found only water, unfortunately. So I do not think I shall do it again here. Perhaps, now, once they have *found* the oil, if they were to ask me to turn the tap on the pipeline to the sea—perhaps I might do that!'

Up a gravel track our convoy passed, slower than usual, for an oil company truck was leading us, and through a rocky pass into the cirque of the Jebel Fahud. It was a strange place. From the track the hills looked perfectly circular (though they assumed quite another shape when you saw them from the air) and we were driving through a flat saucer-like depression in the middle of them. Their summits had been removed by erosion; there were parallel horizontal lines on their surfaces which no doubt carried a message for the geologists, and which reminded me of Brighton Rock. I suppose a few million years before it had all been one big mountain, and the rains which used to fall more profusely in those parts had whittled away the top of it and scooped out the middle. Anyway, it gave an impression of great heat and heartlessness, with its tawny rocks and bare dry hillsides. The effect was portentous, if not ominous; and I did not have to remind myself that this remote and unattractive place might one day be the source of lavish power and wealth almost unimaginable.

The tall steel oil derrick stood haughtily near the eastern edge of the cirque, surrounded by crates, iron things and bits of machinery. When we reached it the whole company dismounted, and while the Sultan was shown around it by the man in charge, sheikhs, walis, imams, Bedouin, slaves and peripheral retainers trooped wonderingly through its legs and over its platforms. When they came to the place where the drill would strike, they leant over the hole and stared at it fixedly. When they passed beneath a steel girder, they fingered it judicially like women examining taffeta at a sale. When the

Sultan descended one ladder, they ascended another: and so this big simple assembly, loaded down with weaponry, swarmed all over the rig, enjoying itself hugely.

'I think the English are very slow,' one man said to me surprisingly. 'The Americans put up their towers much quicker.'

'Perhaps their towers are not so strong,' I suggested vaguely.

'Perhaps. It is true that they have found only water in Dhufar. But I think he who puts his tower up quickest deserves to find the oil!'

I smiled wanly—he had a point: and as I considered the matter I raised my eyes to the platform of the rig to see how the Sultan was enjoying himself. He looked a tiny figure in his turban up there, moving his sandalled feet with a slow and slightly splayed-out motion: and the oil manager, a hefty man, was bending over him, silhouetted against the morning sun, explaining it all. Snatches of conversation reached me, of drills and shafts and girders, cubic tons and pressure ranges: and the Sultan listened gravely.

It was soon time to move on. With careful footsteps Said Bin Taimur descended from the platform and made his way towards the trucks. With a sudden rush the slaves and courtiers hurried from beneath the rig and jumped to their places, the old qadi, breathing heavily, helped along by a little affectionate ribaldry. As I waited in my seat the Sultan passed by with the oil manager, still discussing technicalities. 'I see,' I heard him murmuring as he climbed into his cab: then the engines roared to life, the manager bowed his goodbyes, the slaves settled themselves on the baggage, a solitary goat bayed shakily behind me, and we were away.

5

Into the mountains—with the soldiers—Adam—the falluj—red flags—assemblage at Firq—Nizwa—in the fort—the falluj—Suleiman bin Hamyar

It was a long day's journey from Fahud into the mountains called the Jebel Akhdar, stronghold of the Imam's movement, and the Sultan decided to encamp the next night outside Firq, the village where some rash loyalist, in an heroic moment, had fired the only shot of the military campaign. An escort of the Muscat and Oman Field Force was at Fahud to accompany us there—two or three British officers, in khaki and streaming head-dresses, and a squadron of boyish Arab soldiers recruited on the coast. They were mounted in grey Land Rovers.

'The soldiers tell me', said the Sultan when I went to see him before our departure, 'that they expect to average about fifteen miles an hour. I do not like that, Mr. Morris, as you know. I prefer to travel faster. I think we shall let the escort start earlier and get ahead of us. Will you be ready to start in about two hours' time?'

So the soldiers went off in smart formation, Bren guns at the ready, begoggled like miners. (They had their windscreens flush with their bonnets because, so they told me, a vertical screen encouraged the dust to swirl and eddy around it in a particularly disheartening way. 'Why don't you take the wind-screens off altogether, then?' I asked. 'Nowhere else to put the windscreen wipers.') After the prescribed two hours, spent chiefly in personal and political gossip, we followed them into the highlands at a spanking pace. Soon the country acquired a very different character. As the great mass of Jebel Akhdar loomed in front of us, with its bulky subsidiary ridges like whale-backs against the sky, there began to appear green thickets, wadi beds thick with trees, and a plenitude of struggling friendly foliage. Once I thought I saw an ostrich legging it furiously across the distant gravel; but my driver scoffed at the idea, and I dismissed it as a wishful illusion. Once I thought I observed, away in the distance, the rich palm trees and high walls of some fortified village; the driver scoffed again, but this time he was wrong, for we were approaching the ancient town of Adam, home of the Sultan's ancestors and the westernmost outpost of Oman. This was the beginning of the mountain country, the least-known inhabited area of Arabia.

Colonel S. B. Miles, who visited Adam in 1883 (one of the three Europeans to do so before our present adventures), likened it to an advanced patrol probing towards the Empty Quarter, the outermost breastwork of a settled society. As we approached the place up a long, winding, sporadically green wadi, I agreed that it did indeed stand there as if on the edge of some constantly embattled or endangered territory. The town was surrounded by a high stout wall, here and there strengthened with towers and battlements, so that the deep green of its luxuriant palm trees was skirted by a band of yellowish stone. Beyond it the wadi leading up to the mountains was positively littered with small forts, portly rectangular structures with few windows, blank and bland of manner, and standing all alone among the scrub. They were built according to no system of enfilading or supporting fire, but were dotted about haphaz-ardly, almost as far as the eye could see, rather as (during World War II) ploughs and packing-cases used to be scattered about in English fields to prevent the landing of enemy aircraft.

From one or two of them, and from some meagre windows in the town, small red flags were flying, tokens of allegiance or submission: but this was country of traditional and incessant violence, in which war and revenge were the rules rather than the exceptions, and few of the citizens of Adam ventured upon the walls to see the angry Sultan pass by. The place looked all but deserted: only a handful of black-robed women could be seen cowering beneath the battlements, and two small boys, one wearing a bright russet robe, were the only people to run down the wadi to pay their respects.

It was prayer-time, and we stopped outside the town in an agreeable tree-shaded place where the escort was awaiting us. The Sultan had apparently resolved to make pilgrimage to his ancestral home some other time, for though I saw him inspecting the town through his binoculars, presumably enjoying the same kind of emotions as the Chicago banker revisiting the quaint scenes of his European boyhood, he made no nearer approaches to its walls: possibly doubting its political reliability as the Chicago banker often doubts the efficacy of the parental plumbing. We dismounted and found that only a hundred yards away was a well-cut artificial channel of delicious water, clean and sparkling, if a little warm, and inhabited only by minute endearing fishes. Oman, I was to discover, was crisscrossed with these fallujes, forming an antique but efficient system of irrigation. During several periods of its involved and ill-documented history the country had been ruled by Persians, who had brought with them techniques of irrigation they had perfected at home. Anyone who has flown over the queer brown plain that lies to the south of Teheran will remember the eerie pattern of earth-piles which stretches in complex geometrical precision across the land. These excavatory piles mark the routes of the qanats, forebears of the fallujes, by which water is brought from the mountains to the low farm-lands. Such channels, three or four feet in diameter, have something in common with the London Metropolitan Railway, in that they spend most of their time underground, but part of it on the surface; have regular air-shafts; and can be reached at specific points by flights of stairs, convenient for women with washing to do or men who want to take a bath. Our falluj at Adam was enjoying one of its surface periods, and the Arabs plunged into it with delight, splashing its water all over their faces, soaking their feet in it, drinking it, washing their clothes—doing, in fact, almost everything that a man *can* do with water. To all these travellers water had a mystical quality, as gold or uranium often have to people of other circumstances. As I watched them revelling in it, I remembered the story (probably legendary) of the Sultan at his very grand hotel in London, when he had given such delight to the manager by complimenting him graciously upon the quality of his water. That morning, after so many hundred bleak and waterless miles, I shared this inherited hydrophilia and wallowed in the falluj sensually.

Lush and strange was the country we now entered as, resolutely ignoring Adam, we drove farther into the hills. The groves of trees became more frequent, the little flowering shrubs less embittered. From time to time we passed small walled towns with luscious palm trees and red flags protruding hastily from rooftops. Like the few explorers who had passed this way, and who had generally preferred not to test the fanaticism of these inbred Ibhadi communities, we usually drove by on the other side; and as a rule the population eyed us from behind shuttered windows. At a place called Izz, about which somebody ought to compose a limerick, my driver demonstrated a surprising failure to grasp the first elements of our venture, though by then I thought I had explained the whole thing to him with unmistakable clarity. 'Is that town there', said he, 'owned by the Sultan or by some other governor?' 'There is no other governor,' I said piously, feeling like the wali from Dhufar, 'only the Sultan.' 'Good,' said the driver, 'very good.'

All the same, it would obviously be untrue to say that the Sultan was being received by his Omani subjects with any great display of enthusiasm. We were now in fairly thickly populated country, and here and there knots of Arabs, underfed and dishevelled, lined the track to see us pass. One or two of the quicker ones had seized little red flags which they waved half-heartedly: but most of them stood there with striking apathy, staring open-mouthed as the truck with the flag stormed by, peering myopically at the Sultan, greeting the rest of us with an almost universal vacuity of expression. Occasionally some urchin performed a diffident wave; and sometimes an old zealot with a white beard, summoning a spark of defiance, managed some gesture of distaste, a spit or an unfriendly movement of his hands, when he realized there were Christians in the convoy. 'Why should we help you?' some of the Omani Bedouin had asked Wilfred Thesiger, during one of his brilliant journeys a few years before. 'If we help you other Christians will come in motor-cars, looking for oil, and they will take our land away from us.' Some such suspicions, no doubt, passed through the minds of these fierce old worthies as they assembled their saliva.

The flags grew more common as we travelled up the valley, but had a hastily improvised air about them, rather as though the householders, seeing the distant dust of the Sultan's cortège, had grabbed a few old red coverlets and a scarlet petticoat or two, and torn them into shape. Here and there nothing red had been at hand, the poor housewife had ransacked her rag-bag helplessly, the irate husband had stormed and fumed, and in the end they had compromised with a bluish-greenish pillowcase, or even (in one instance) with a tattered piece of unambiguous yellow. The place was thick with flags; but a heavy airless haze hung over the valley, in the heat of the late morning, and they hung there limply and forlorn.

They looked, somehow, especially inadequate at a village called Ma'amir, which we reached in the afternoon after winding a way through many a wadi and thicket, past innumerable forts, watch-towers and other warlike structures. This place presented an intriguingly troglodytic effect, for its stone-built houses clustered around, and sometimes seemed part of, a large pyramidal rock, on the top of which some wayward talent had stuck the smallest imaginable red flag, about the size of a lady's handkerchief. I found it impossible to tell where the houses began and the rock ended, or whether various holes I saw were the uninviting windows of upstairs rooms or actual caves in the hillside. The inhabitants of Ma'amir had turned out *en masse*, dressed in a variety of flowing robes, turbans and fighting equipment that defied accurate analysis: and a peculiarly surly and disgruntled lot they looked, as if the rock had entered their souls as effectively as it had entered their back parlours.

At last we found that only a minor ridge or two of fine craggy rocks separated us from the Jebel Akhdar, now standing imposing above us; and presently we saw in the middle distance, masked by palm groves and outer works, the round stone tower of the fort at Firq, from which had issued that memorable rifle-shot. We were on the very edge of the Imam's fastnesses, and we pitched camp that evening wondering how many of his henchmen would arrive next morning to swear fealty and how many were oiling their rifles in the surrounding hills.

But though the soldiers kept watch throughout the night, no screaming tribesmen charged us from the mountains: on the contrary, almost before dawn the first deferential citizens arrived to bend their knees before the Sultan, and the day (which had possessed agreeable possibilities of antique violence) degenerated into something like the Queen's Birthday in Cairo, when the ladies in their straws and summer frocks, and the men in their tight white suits, arrive importantly to sign their names in the Embassy book. The comings and goings were varied and incessant, and the characters who crossed that unlikely stage well worth the watching.

Not the least notable was a tall man dressed in white, wearing on his head a sort of turban with streaming ends, and on his

face an expression of gloriously incongruous English benevolence, rather as though, perhaps in company with the Sultan's father-in-law, he was about to judge the onions at an
agricultural show. This was the Sultan's English Foreign
Minister or Wazir, a successor to Bertram Thomas in that
gratifying office, who lived in Muscat and had been flown to a
hastily-contrived airstrip in the valley outside Firq. He carried
an old-fashioned ciné-camera, bringing a touch of Chaplin to
our proceedings; and often he retired to his tent to produce a
communiqué, couched in language of almost mediaeval vehe-
mence, describing the progress of the Sultan's affairs.

But no less individual, in their own ways, were the coveys of
Arabs who trooped in from the earliest light of morning. I was
awakened, while it was still half-dark, by an excited Arabic
jabbering and chattering outside my tent: and disengaging
myself with difficulty from my blankets, for it had been a cold
night, I crawled to the entrance in time to see a huge misty
company of shapeless figures, all draperies and turbans, seep-
ing through the gloom towards the Sultan's tent. For a brief
moment I thought, with a pleasurable pang of excitement, that
they were going to hurl themselves upon it, but their voices
soon made it clear that they were friendly disposed. I wondered
how they would be welcomed, for I knew the Sultan used to
enjoy tea and biscuits quietly in bed before getting up; and sure
enough, there suddenly sprang out of nowhere three or four
black stalwarts, wide awake and heavily armed, to dissuade the
approaching procession from its purposes and turn it around
on its tracks. Without much protest it shambled away again,
and settled down in the gloom in a huge hollow square, to
await the Sultan's pleasure.

When I had breakfasted and dressed, I found those Arabs
still sitting there patiently, joined by the wali, the qadi and the
Yal Wahiba sheikhs. They sat on their heels silently with their
rifles pointing to the sky, staring vacantly into the middle distance. Their faces were poor, pinched and pocked with diseases, and their bodies were bent and wizened. Many were

hunchbacks. Some were dwarfs. One blind man was helped to a position on his crutches. The children around the perimeter of this assemblage (some of them, indeed, sitting unabashed in the middle of it) were characterized by such receding chins and foreheads, by such pitiably thin bodies, such big protruding goggle-eyes, that they reminded me irresistibly of those little creatures, only just removed from inanimation, that you find in the middle of cuckoo-spit. A few women in black hovered timorously in the distance, and the high scratchy timbre of their voices sometimes grated upon the silence. All in all, it was a sad and oafish company that sat in the square that morning.

The hours passed; the Sultan busied himself, perhaps with a view to establishing his unassailable dignity, with other matters; and from time to time new arrivals joined the waiting supplicants. Portentous sheikhs appeared dressed resplendently. An old dignitary toppled in on a camel, a cloud of servants billowing about its hind legs, and a space of honour was cleared for him near the wali as he creaked and groaned his way to the square on two gnarled walking-sticks. A coffee-pourer trod delicately to the inside of the concourse and moved around it flourishing pot and cups—the Arabs, in the Bedouin manner, holding their cups out straight if they wanted more, or wiggling them disparagingly if they had drunk enough.

Then quite suddenly, and by that indefinable method of communication, part suggestion, part instinct, that is peculiar to the Arabs, intelligence arrived that the Sultan was ready for them. They rose to their feet, grasping their weapons and straightening their clothes, and moved off towards the tent, led majestically by the wali and the Yal Wahiba sheikhs (who looked, in this raggety company, bolder and more splendid than ever). I watched them go, and presently the Sultan emerged from his tent in his fawn robes, his sword at his side, and I saw him engulfed by his respectful (or remorseful) subjects.

'You'd better come with us in the front car,' said one of the officers, 'then you can get shot at first!' So when we moved off towards Firq I travelled in the first vehicle, followed by the flag truck (in which the Bedouin guide looked more depressed than ever, and was also complaining of tooth-ache) and then by the Sultan. The lingering crowd around our camp, now waving us a gloomy good-bye, had certainly seemed heavily overawed by the Sultan, and even more, perhaps, by the weight of his military forces. But the soldiers still cherished a secret hope that some ornery old sheikh of the hills, inspired by the long historical tradition of Omani intransigence, would order his bondsmen to attempt a counter-attack or assassination. The Imam was now known to have returned to his own village, deeper in the mountains, where he had been allowed to remain unmolested: but his brother Talib, whom the Wazir liked to call the 'evil genius' of the case, was still at large. There was a Buchanesque touch to this man's activities which warmed me to him. He had himself directed the fight on the other side of the mountains, I learnt, and when his chief fort there had fallen he had made a successful get-away, allegedly taking with him a number of boxes of gold. Anyone who caught him, the Sultan's government had announced, would be handsomely rewarded by the State and would also take possession of this treasure (a declaration which, I must confess, made me wonder whether the bit about the boxes had not a slight touch of the mythical to it). But the resourceful Talib had vanished utterly, through the unknown crannies of the mountains, and the latest rumour was that he had left the Batinah coast by dhow and was on his way to Saudi Arabia, pursued by gunboats and customs launches.

So constant were the inter-tribal wars which racked the social history of Oman that each town was fortified against its neighbours, and sometimes individual homes were militarized rather in the manner of Scottish baronial houses (indeed I think the highlanders of Oman had a good deal in common with their Scottish counterparts); so that approaching such a place as Firq, through its many strong-points and watch-towers, was rather like approaching some aboriginal Maginot Line. But the

loopholes and battlements were unmanned, and from the top of
the principal fort a red flag fluttered reassuringly. It was a day
of unusual clarity. The mountains ahead of us, often smeared
with haze, were clear-cut that morning, and the groves of
pomegranates, bananas and sour oranges that swathed and
beautified Firq were vividly green against the blue sky. Most of
the inhabitants hung about their windows and gateways
uncertainly, scarcely venturing into the highway, as if, like
citizens of a rebellious colony, they expected some form of
collective punishment: we did not stop in the narrow street of
the village, however, but pressed on to Nizwa.

We were an impressive spectacle by now, for along the way
various segments of the Sultan's army, having taken part in the
original advance, had joined our convoy; and when we crossed
a wadi full of fresh water, I looked behind to see the trucks and
Land Rovers splashing through it splendidly, disintegrating
the reflected palms, mountains and white clouds that floated
bewitchingly upon its surface. As we approached the Imam's
capital, among its spacious groves, the knots of bystanders
thickened and the sense of excitement grew; until at last we
drove up a dry wadi bed into the town to find crowds of white-
robed Arabs awaiting our arrival on tiptoe, holding sticks and
rifles, with swarms of women in bright orange dresses, like a
shifting sea of orange peel, twittering together in the back-
ground. The red flag of Muscat rounded the bend; the Sultan
immediately followed; and pandemonium broke loose. At the
head of the wadi stood the celebrated round fort of Nizwa, solid
and immense, the strongest in Oman; and suddenly from its
battlements there billowed a deafening explosion as an ancient
Portuguese gun, left behind by those conquerors three centuries before, roared a welcome. So powerful was the charge
inserted by the gunners, in their excesses of precautionary enthusiasm, that the cannon at once blew up, severely injuring an
aged onlooker: but undaunted they turned to other artillery
and throughout that morning our activities were punctuated by
cataclysmic detonations from the fort, so violent that pieces of

the structure often flew off with the shock, and once I seriously thought the whole thing was going to collapse on top of us. All around us, as we drove up the wadi, grave-faced tribesmen raised their weapons to the air and fired *feux de joie*, and the erratic crackling of these rifle-shots mingled richly with shouts of incoherent greeting, the excited muttering of a thousand Arabs, the squeaky bird-like converse of the women, the roar of our engines, the hooting of our horns, and the shattering explosions of the cannon. White smoke wreathed the fortress tower, and through it figures with ramrods could indistinctly be seen, as in prints of nineteenth-century naval battles.

A group of elders, maintaining their severe decorum with difficulty, moved forward from the steps of the fort as the convoy arrived. The ruler, dismounting as grandly from his dusty truck as any be-plumed emperor from his landau, was looking his most magnificent. His multi-coloured turban was impeccably wound. His aba was gorgeously edged in gold. His golden sword-hilt sparkled. ('Very posh', I wrote in my notebook.) For the first time in living memory a Sultan of Muscat was in Oman, and the occasion was obviously not lost upon Said bin Taimur.

In a moment he had vanished among the tribesmen, pressing about him to shout protestations of unwavering loyalty. He disappeared entirely in a morass of rifles, flags, beards and turbans that bore him swiftly up the shallow steps of the fortress and into its courtyards. By the time I had dismounted from my Land Rover, he was gone. I fought my way through a mass of curious citizens, including a large number of small, peaky boys bearing muskets of unnaturally large size. An English colonel carrying a camera reached a friendly hand down to me and helped me up the steps of the fort, now jammed with a confusion of eager sheikhs. 'What an extraordinary affair!' said he. 'The last two shots I entirely forgot to take my lens cap off!' I sympathized with him through the din, for earlier in my journey I had taken six or seven pictures without having a film in my camera: and then moved slowly, making use of my elbows, through the gateway of the fort. A squat Portuguese cannon stood in the shadow of the gate (it was said to have come from the old island stronghold of Hormuz, at the entrance to the Persian Gulf, described by a fifteenth-century traveller as 'a port which has no equal on the face of the earth'); but the occupants of the citadel had evidently determined, once the Imam had deserted them, upon a policy of the frankest kind of appeasement, for the courtyard was gay with bunting and small flags. Many-coloured strings of flags ran across it, and pieces of red bunting fluttered from every protrusion. Beneath these decorations seethed a multitude of Arabs, young and old, who had ridden in from the far corners of the interior to swear allegiance to the Sultan while the going was good. Some sat in the customary hollow square. Some dangled their legs over the edges of parapets. Some wandered about in two and threes. Some battered at a big wooden door, studded with nails, in a vain attempt to gain admittance to some inner fastness. Some sat on the floor cogitating. Like the inhabitants of Firq, they were a poor, thin, weak-limbed people; every other sheikh suffered from some eye disease, and there were hunchbacks and cripples innumerable.

A few of these men were unfriendly as I shouldered my way through them, turning their backs upon me or muttering obscure and so far ineffectual imprecations under their breath: but most of them were extremely helpful. I found my way to a kind of council chamber at one side of the courtyard, with lattice windows overlooking the street, inside which were sitting, despite an almost unbearable incidence of flies, a group of sober and genial sheikhs.

'Where is the Sultan?' said I.

'He is inside the fort. Knock on the door, and you will be admitted.'

'But the sheikhs are already knocking at it, and nobody opens it.'

'Never mind! Shout in a loud voice: "Make way for the Sahib!" and they will open the door.'

I thanked them; we exchanged good wishes; and I pushed a passage through the courtyard to the door. To my astonishment the medley of sheikhs which had been hammering upon it instantly gave way and shouted loudly: 'O keeper of the gate! Open at once for the Sahib! Open the gate!' The door opened immediately, and not another soul tried to squeeze in as I entered. Instead those strange men laughed, patted me kindly on the back, exchanged a quip or two, and waited until the door was firmly closed again before resuming their clamorous demands for entry.

Inside, far from finding the Sultan sitting in state, I was faced with a series of shadowy passages, down which, through sundry windows and openings, shafts of sunlight passed romantically. I picked my passage and advanced down it, and soon found myself in a small inner courtyard, with a similar throng of sheikhs hammering on a similar door. They smiled, wished me peace, and yelled: 'Open up, the Sahib wants to enter!'; and when the door instantly opened they fell back a little and exchanged the time of day with the door-keeper, whose heavily bearded face peered out from the interior gloom as I bent my head and passed beneath the low lintel of the gate.

The Wazir of Muscat and Oman was re-winding his ciné-camera and chatting with the commander of the Muscat and Oman Field Force, a former Indian Army officer. 'The Sultan?' they said. 'He's upstairs. I shouldn't go barging in, but if you go up that staircase there you can catch a glimpse of him. Mind the steps, they're very narrow!'

I climbed a steep staircase, nearly falling backwards down it, to the scarcely repressed amusement of the field force commander, when there was a particularly devastating blast from the cannon in the keep; and there in a long ornate hall, maintained in fine condition, the Sultan was receiving the humble submissions of his mountain chiefs. In a long rectangle those picturesque worthies sat, rifles and canes in hand, saying not a word: and at their head was a Sultan entirely new to me. He sat there still as an idol in his splendid robes, cross-legged, impassive, and into his eyes there had entered an expression of tremendous hauteur and authority. His head was held aristocratically high. The faint suspicion of a sneer curled the corners of his mouth. His attitude was one of languid but relentless command. The sheikhs, sitting there in the chill of his supremacy, hardly dared to fidget.

Nizwa, once the centre of thriving textile and ironworking industries, the prosperous capital of Oman, had clearly gone down in the world. So dwarfish, diseased and simian were its inhabitants, so fly-ridden its suk, that the Sultan (having established his ascendancy and ordered the immediate erection of a medical centre) decided to set up his headquarters outside the town. About two miles to the north there was a wide level plain, enclosed by hills and guarded by a solitary strong-point on a ridge. There the army had already parked its vehicles, and two young English soldiers, lent by the British Army, had set up a small wireless transmitter; and there the royal tents were pitched. There was never a better place for paying allegiances to sultans. On this plain (so they said) the armies of Haroun al-Raschid had encamped during their campaign in Oman eleven hundred years before; and here throughout the generations the warring factions of that incorrigible country had gathered their camels, their flags and their ponderous muskets to fight out their ridiculous squabbles. It felt as though a thousand battles had been fought there; but somehow I sensed in my bones that not a proportionate number of men had been killed. Directly above the plain, rising grandly above a ripple of palm trees, stood the mountain mass of Jebel Akhdar—the Green Mountain. It did not seem very green. On the contrary, it was bare and tawny, and looked watchful and implacable. It reaches a height of nearly 10,000 feet, making it one of the highest mountains in Arabia. Some of the Arabs say they have seen it 'covered with salt', presumably meaning that for a few weeks of a savagely severe winter the mountain is snow-capped. (Looking at the map as I lay in my tent, I assumed that these Omani highlands were an extension of the Zagros Mountains

of Persia, which were separated from them only by the narrow
Straits of Hormuz, and which were in the news then because
they formed the eastern defence line of the western system of
alliances. Obvious though this had been to generations of geographers, as well as to me, it was apparently not true; for the
advanced geological view seems to be that the two chains are
unconnected, and that the Omani mountains run away to the
south-east and into the sea. One or two of my ruminations at
Nizwa, concerning high strategy, the links of history, Abbas
Shah and the delicate poets of Shiraz, were therefore rudely
invalidated later.)

Here the Sultan settled down, and there began two days of
constant comings and goings, ceremonials, demonstrations of
loyalty, parades and pageantries. Camp was pitched in the
early afternoon, and before tea the Sultan inspected the
soldiers of his little army, which, though indeed it had escaped
ordeal by fire, had certainly behaved itself commendably. The
soldiers were drawn up in a square. The British officers stood
stiffly in the middle, the stoutest of them performing the
introductions. The Wazir, who lived his official life with a
disarming lack of pomposity, happily prepared his camera.
From the distance there was a faint confused hum of Arab
shouts, chants and laughter; but in the plain all was silent as
the Sultan stepped royally forward to address his troops. His
speech was delivered in Arabic of classical impeccability, and
his voice rose and fell in graceful cadences. I much enjoyed,
though, a translation of it kindly given to me afterwards by a
Muscati soldier who had learnt English at a mission school,
and whose version therefore had an unexpectedly evangelical
tone to it:

'Here unto me O ye soldiers for I am very happy in this day
to you and all your officers. For the thing which I was asking
for a long time. The people who wants to get the foreigner in
your and mine home land. Again to thank you all. Be known O
ye soldiers though I am far away from you for ye see your
officers just like you have seen me. Though you are not see me

in person but your officers daily are reporting unto me of your good doing so also your officers are very thankful to you. Your love in me is very cordiality. The way you hear me and obey me please also hear to your officers and be obedient unto them. I will ask and plead to Almighty God for your long living life.'

The ceremony ended with a smart 'present arms' and an announcement that the soldiers would get a bonus of a month's pay. The troops moved off, a little disappointed that they had not been given a permanent rise in wages—they earned less than oil company coolies, and some of them had no boots—but flattered at such an encomium and no doubt planning some brief commemorative orgy (if you can have such a thing in so begrudging an environment). Almost at once the first of the local penitents and supplicants appeared around the corner. Some were slovenly men with sticks and tattered robes. Some were grand and self-satisfied. A very small boy in filthy rags, with horrible festering and decaying sores around his eyes, wandered into camp carrying a dirty linen bag and asked fearfully for the Sultan, to be pushed away, reviled or ignored by all those smug fellow-supplicants he had the temerity to approach. Eighteen camel-men, their rifles across their backs, rode up the valley at a fast trot, draperies streaming, the heads of their animals held high and proud. Sheikhs innumerable and indescribable arrived with bands of wretched vagabond followers, as different from our lordly Yal Wahiba chiefs as a tinned cream cheese from a Stilton. There were too many people for one of those silent ruminative squares such as had been established at Firq: instead a number of them sprang into existence, quite autonomous and separate, and the coffee-pourers multiplied, and sprang from square to square, from camp-fire to sheikhly group, with great agility and enthusiasm. From time to time some person of consequence—a 'personality', as it is expressed both in Arabic and in the jargon of television—was admitted to the Sultan's tent and emerged a few moments later looking chastened but relieved; and at prayer-time the whole lot of them, no doubt aware of the

Sultan's piety, sprang to their devotions with an eagerness that might have seemed, to a more cynical observer, a trifle unconvincing.

All these sheikhly affairs lasted for two days, and during this time, tiring a little of the courtly flavour of it all, I wandered agreeably about that old battle-field, through the shady palm groves that surrounded it and across the ridges that overlooked it on every side. This was all but virgin country to westerners, and a fine, fertile place it was. Nizwa commanded an important junction of trade routes, and dominated the gateway into the Jebel Akhdar; with its four streams it was probably the best-watered town in Oman. It was the key-point of the national history, at once the Hastings, the Westminster and the Canterbury of Oman; where successive conquerors had fought their decisive battles; where the rulers of Oman had directed their governments; and where in the eighth century Abdullah bin Ibadh first preached the contentious doctrines of his schism. The palms were lavish. The wadis ran blue and sparkling. The big round fort, begun in the fifteenth century, loomed pompously among the narrow streets, and rows of old houses stood square and symmetrical beside the main thoroughfare, looking (with their rectangular outlines, their terraced dignity and their great wooden doors) not unlike the canal-side houses of Amsterdam.

During the first afternoon I climbed to the fort which protected our camping ground. There was no sign of life in it, but as I climbed the hillside in the heat a little unsuspected door opened in its flank and a soldier emerged to greet me. 'Welcome!' said he. 'Come and see our fort!' I did so with pleasure, for it was typical of the sturdy strong-points erected by the tumultuous Omani tribes in the course of their constant Montague-and-Capulet disturbances—which often divided hamlets into irreconcilable quarters, and sometimes even made one part of a household totally unacceptable to the other. I found it to be not only strong, but unusually well-designed and self-sufficient. The door led only to a small cavity in the stone-work. From it a long dark cylindrical tunnel led vertically to the upperworks, and up this gloomy place you must swarm up on a rope. I squeezed into the thing and pulled myself up it clumsily, groping against the brickwork with my feet and imagining clearly the quantities of boiling oil which might by now be descending upon me if an enemy stood at the top. Faintly above me I could see a pale smudge, and presently it resolved itself into a cheerful bareheaded Arab face, peering down at me from the platform above. 'Ha, ha!' it said. 'He's not so fat as our Major!' (This being a reference, not perhaps in the best of taste, to the physical inability of their squadron commander to inspect that particular outpost.) The flies at the top were intolerable. Clouds of them swarmed into every cranny and covered the soldiers' hampers of food, stored in lockers in the walls, with a beastly black pall. But the view over the valley was splendid. Nizwa was couched in palm trees below us; the mountains were behind; and to the west I fancied I could see a distant sandy streak of the Empty Quarter.

Nobody could take this fort, said the soldiers complacently, cleaning their rifles with a determined air. They had food up there, and water, and ammunition; and pointing through a low doorway in the battlements they showed me, affixed to the external wall of the fort, fifty feet or more above the ground, a small framework contraption which fulfilled the purposes of a lavatory. Thus all the essentials of defensive existence had been considered by the designer of this admirable structure. I chatted with the soldiers for a moment or two and then, sling-ing my camera around my neck, jumped on to the rope and slid dizzily down into the void. The door banged behind me as I walked into the open air: and the fort seemed as empty and lifeless as ever, as no doubt it had to many a careless marauder sneaking up in the darkness of an Arabian night to be greeted with curses and oil.

In the evening, the camp still simmering with penitents and grandees, I walked across to the main falluj of Nizwa. It ran through a flat piece of ground outside the town which was dotted with square stone buildings, some of them prayer-houses, some of them washing-huts, some of them little forts for the protection of the falluj. The water channel ran underground here, on its way from its mountain sources to the town, but there were three or four stone-built openings and flights of steps into its interior. I chose my steps, and there at the bottom in the half-light the falluj ran bubbling by. Above me was a little square of blue sky. The water flowed away into its tunnel mysteriously, reminding me of that underground channel at Oxford, called the Trill Mill Stream, through which T. E. Lawrence once sailed on his stomach in a canoe. Removing my clothes, I lay in the water deliciously. The day was still and quiet, but from down the tunnel I could hear the gay voices of girls doing their washing at the next staircase, with splashes and laughing repartee, a little distorted by the echoing cavity of the falluj. The water was very warm, and in it hundreds of little fishes swam about and nibbled at my toes.

It was said to have medicinal qualities, and certainly had its effect on me. Within an hour or two I was lying in my tent helpless and exhausted, thanking my good fortune that I was not on duty at the top of the fort. The wise Indian doctor of the field force found me in this condition, abjured me briskly to eat nothing whatsoever, gave me fifteen pills which he told me to swallow one after the other in the swiftest possible succession, wished me a happy Christmas (for it was Christmas Eve) and cured me overnight. People often felt that, it appeared, after a bathe in a falluj. It must be awful for the fishes.

By the end of the day nearly all the petty sheikhs of that country had established relations with the Sultan, presumably to their mutual satisfaction, for there were no executions and most of the eminent locals, as they trotted off on their camels or hobbled away among their screens of followers, looked, on the whole, relieved. The great man of the area, however, the most dangerous to the Sultan's sovereignty, the most notorious for his stubborn lawlessness, had not yet put in an appearance. Suleiman bin Hamyar, lord of the Jebel Akhdar, had let it be known, through obscure channels, that he would submit to the Sultan; but with such characters you never knew, and the soldiers and courtiers awaited his arrival with anxious concern. The Imam Ghalib (unlike his immediate predecessor, an able and respected man), was alleged to be weak and vacillating, as well as traitorous, and in Bahrain I had asked whether there was any *eminence grise*, apart from the 'evil genius' Talib, who stood strong behind the Imamate in the Oman highlands. Yes, they said, there was: Suleiman, sheikh of the Bani Riyam and undisputed ruler of the Jebel Akhdar. This formidable old warrior lived in the heart of the mountains, and could if he wished offer the Sultan a stout resistance or launch some exhilarating forays into our valley. His hill country was virtually unknown, and its few rocky tracks would certainly offer heavy going for the vehicles of the field force. (Only one organized army had ever penetrated those heights—the Persians, in the tenth century, stormed the mountains with great losses and fought a victorious battle on their summit, 9,000 feet up. Many of them, strangely enough, liked the place so much, despite this bloody introduction to it, that they settled on the slopes of the Jebel Akhdar; and their descendants live there still.)

Suleiman bin Hamyar came of rugged stock. When Sir Percy Cox travelled through Oman in 1905 he met the father of the present intransigent, who promptly tried to blackmail him by demanding safe-conduct money. Forty-five years later Wilfred Thesiger met the son, and described him graphically as 'a powerful if not very congenial personality'. He was certainly a man of character, reported to be less fanatical and narrow-minded than some of his associates—a trait which had put him at logger-heads with the previous Imam, a man of stringent principles—and correspondingly, I suppose, more dangerous to the Sultan. His word was known to be law in the mountains, and rumour had it that he had been in regular correspondence with the Saudi Arabians, for whom he could act as an unusually potent if unpredictable puppet. At one time he acquired for himself, and proudly used, the resonant but ill-documented title of King of Nebhkaniya. His figure marched through the political discussions of Muscat inexorably, like a mountain spectre.

So we eyed the mountain with interest, half hoping to see battalions of wild camel-men emerging from its recesses, flaunting the flag of the Imamate. During the night, indeed, word did reach the camp that Suleiman was about to embark upon such an adventure, and that his supporters might be upon us at any moment. The soldiers were aroused from their beds, the gun-sites were alerted, the men in the fort barricaded their door and peered into the night, and even the mountain howitzers, I believe, had the wrappings removed from their Edwardian mechanisms: but nothing happened, and the only riders to appear, in the early morning, were yet another company of countrymen coming to demonstrate their deference.

Eventually, though, Suleiman bin Hamyar did appear, and in a suitably individual manner. Next day, at a convenient and gentlemanly mid-morning hour, we saw approaching us from the mountains a moving pillar of dust, quite unlike those surging clouds that had, in the past few days, heralded the arrival of so many camel trains. It was either a tribal band of unprecendented character, we thought, or something totally different, peculiar to the Green Mountains, like a camel-drawn dray or a sledge, pulled by mules, such as you sometimes see in the southern states of America. But as the pillar grew nearer, and we were able to look into the middle of it, as you might look into the interior of a small tornado, we saw that it was something infinitely more astonishing: a perfectly good, well-kept, fairly modern American convertible. It had never occurred to anybody before that there was a single car in these remote regions; and indeed Suleiman's, presumably supplied by his Saudi well-wishers, was the only one. The sight of it careening out of the mountains towards us, bouncing recklessly over the rough track, was wonderfully inconsequential and inspiriting. The roof of the car was closed, but on the boot there sat a negro slave, armed with a rifle, with his feet sticking through the back window into the inside of the car; and when it stopped outside the camp this slave jumped off like lightning, as promptly and neatly as any duke's footman, and opened the door with a flourish. Three sheikhly figures were sitting inside, rather cramped, and they stepped out slowly, shaking out their grand clothes like ball dresses, and carrying their weapons rather as a lady might clasp her jewelled evening bag.

Two of them were young men, serving perhaps as aides-de-camp, callow of face and feeble of physique: but the third, who swaggered behind them like some great Sicilian bandit, was Suleiman bin Hamyar himself. The Sultan's slaves, trim in their blue sweaters, ran light-footed to meet the visitors and asked them to wait; and I walked across to greet them. I shall always remember the moment, for the old sheikh rose to his feet with an expression that I can only describe as being of unfathomable foxiness, suggesting to me instantly some infinitely clever beast in Æsop, about to hoodwink a lion, goat or slow-witted bird. ('O Lord', runs a Bedouin prayer, 'have mercy upon Mohammed and me, but on no one else besides.') Suleiman was a big man with a powerful face, rather Dickensian in concept, and a triangular grey beard. On his head was a twisted blue and white turban. His aba was blue, gold-edged and filmy. In his hand was a cane with a carved end, and in his belt a curved Omani dagger of splendid ostentation, which I greatly coveted. The old rogue seemed keen to have his picture taken, but as he prepared to pose word arrived that the Sultan was waiting for him; and hastily assuming an expression of unutterable innocence, Suleiman followed the slaves to the presence. My own instinct told me that this fine scoundrel should be instantly decapitated, for the good of the Sultan and the sterling area, if so ill-matched a pair of causes might be placed in partnership; but I was rather glad, all the same, when he reappeared from the interview intact, and drove away into his mountains with only minor (and I felt sure temporary) modifications of his manner.

So Christmas Day came. I went to the Sultan's tent to wish him happiness, and found him fragrant with an especially pervasive perfume, redolent of bowers and Oriental delights. But far from embarking that afternoon upon any languorous erotic exercises, the Sultan was treated to a military demonstration by his troops, and the old cockpit rang to the sound of mortar bombs and rifle-fire. If Suleiman and his friends heard the din from their closeted fortress houses in the mountains, or if the Imam heard it in the sad obscurity of his village, it no doubt confirmed their convictions about the better part of valour.

6

The Sultan was a man of pronounced personal and hereditary pride (there was a story of some unhappy altercation when he was inadvertently invited, though a sovereign ruler, to the coronation of Queen Elizabeth II) and he was understandably pleased by the turn of events. Not a chieftain, from the redoubtable Suleiman to the meanest factional demagogue, now defied his newly-imposed authority in Oman. On both sides of the mountain range his enemies had surrendered or submitted. For the first time in the twentieth century a sultan had visited Nizwa, the ancient capital of the interior; and for the first time since before the first world war a sultan might be said to be the effective ruler of his entire sultanate. Whether this rule was *de jure* as well as *de facto* was, of course, another matter, and one that probably did not unduly exercise the minds of either the Sultan's liegemen or his direct opponents: but at least evidence had been found which handsomely confirmed the allegations about Saudi activities in Oman, and about the Imam's separatist ambitions. According to Ghalib's chief askari (still presiding, like the sergeant-major of some disbanded regiment, over the fort at Nizwa) a consignment of more than 2,000 rifles had reached the Imam only a month or two before, together with 60,000 rounds of ammunition. Quantities of such supplies had been smuggled through the mountains from the east coast. Others had, without doubt, reached Nizwa by way of Buraimi. A few days before our descent upon Oman an unfortunate Arab had arrived at Buraimi with a camel-train loaded with rifles, for delivery to the Imam with Saudi compliments: poor man, he had been so long crossing the eastern desert that he had not heard about the British occupation of Buraimi, and marched into that oasis all unsuspecting, flourishing his bill of lading. There was also found, among the mass of correspondence in the fly-blown fortress, a letter to the Imam from Colonel Nasser of Egypt, at that time the principal anti-western force in the Middle East, whose recent agreement to buy arms from Communist Czechoslovakia had plunged the whole region into crisis. When the Imam had tried to enter the Arab League as an independent sovereign, Egypt had joined Saudi Arabia in supporting his pretensions—though I am told the relevant meeting of the league council was adjourned to allow members to look up Oman in the atlas. Nasser's letter therefore assured Ghalib of his good wishes, and conveniently provided the Sultan with grist for his political mill. (Even in Omani affairs historical precedents were to be found. Napoleon, when *he* was the most ambitious man in the Middle East, wrote to the then Imam of Oman from Egypt to assure him of his good intentions; and when a later Imam sent a gift of Arab horses to the President of the French Republic, in 1849, one Paris publication observed: 'The Imam's envoy has just left Paris after having been received in mediocre fashion by the Government, which does not seem to know who the Imam is.')

Glowing with pleasure at all these circumstances, the Wazir wrote a number of *communiqués*, admirably suited to Arab polemical tastes, which were radioed to Bahrain and thence published to a somewhat apathetic world. 'Sultan Said bin Taimur bin Feisal bin Turki,' it was announced grandiloquently, 'eighth Sultan of Muscat and Oman since the establishment of the Al Bu Said dynasty by the great Said bin Sultan bin Ahmed el Imam some 200 years ago, and eleventh successive Ruler of Oman from the Al Bu Said family, arrived in Nizwa on 9th Jomada el Ula 1375 and 24th December 1955 to receive the homage of his loyal subjects and the submission of those who had conspired against him. He had driven about 700 miles, pioneering a new route skirting south of the Rub el Khali, to reach Nizwa from his South-West Province of Dhufar. Sheikh Ghalib bin Ali, who had put forward pretensions of independence of the Sultan, left Nizwa on the advance of the Sultan's forces and is said to have made public renunciation of his pretensions before leaving. His brother Talib, the former pretender's evil genius and principal tool and go-between of foreign instigation of conspiracy, is on the run. Letters expressing relief, pleasure and loyalty are pouring into Nizwa from local notables and villagers. The prominent conspirator Suleiman bin Hamyar of the Jebel Akhdar area has made his humble submission and awaits the Sultan's pleasure.' A loyal sheikh of the Al Hathira tribe (he had become its chief shortly before by deposing his uncle, an Imam's man) was installed in Nizwa as the Sultan's representative with a force of 300 camel-men; and a squadron of the field force prepared to take up permanent station outside the town, its commander delighted at the prospect of such independent tranquil duty.

So the ruler now looked, if possible, even grander than before, and we left Nizwa basking in his elation. The Arabs lining our track seemed a little surer of themselves, now they had digested the examples of their leaders, and waved flags at us with a new gusto. In Nizwa a farewell blast of the cannon startled my driver so violently that he almost precipitated us into the wadi. At Firq the inhabitants now ventured out of their houses into the street, delighted at getting off so easily, and one pleasant woman reached into my window as we passed and gave me an orange. There was no relaxation to be detected, indeed, in the sour faces of the troglodytes, still standing beside their rock at Ma'amir: but never a spit did I see that day between Nizwa and Izz. Adam still seemed deserted, and only five lean and probing boys, including one jet-black negro, emerged to poke their sharp noses into our affairs. In a day's hard driving we were out of the mountains, and driving northwest along their fringes, between the highlands and the desert.

About seventy miles north of Fahud, set amongst some of the richest date and fruit groves in Oman, stood the small and once notorious bazaar town of Ibri. It had enjoyed a long chequered history. For generations it was famous as a thieves' market, in which the innumerable bandits who roamed that particular part of the country could find a sale for their booty. It also had a record of fanatical xenophobia. The first two Europeans to reach it, the naval officers Wellsted and Whitelock, were driven off with stones when they arrived there in 1836. The third, Colonel Miles, nearly lost his possessions at the hands of robbers in 1885. The fourth, Sir Percy Cox, found the townspeople friendly in 1905, but was shot at outside the place; and in 1949 Thesiger, travelling in disguise in the most daring of Omani explorations, thought it wiser to skirt so troublesome a village altogether.

Ibri had always been a centre of tribal rivalries of the most vicious and tenacious kind, and was once so infested by criminals and torn by vendettas that people were afraid to sleep in their houses, preferring to spend the nights in the open where one man could not be distinguished from another. It was the chief settlement of the Dhahira district, a region that owed no very definable loyalty either to the Imam or to the Sultan, and it had long been inhabited by severely puritanical Wahabis of the same Islamic sect which ruled Saudi Arabia. Its future was therefore of interest to the Sultan. Not only did it look fruitful ground for Saudi intrigue, but it was also dangerously close to the hazy margin of the frontier. The British, too, took an especial interest in Ibri because of its proximity to Fahud. The town had accordingly been occupied by the field force; a garrison had been stationed on its outskirts; and the Sultan was now riding to set his seal upon the action as Claudius once followed the Roman legions into England to earn the title of 'Britannicus'.

Occasionally, on our way there, we passed some small palm-girded village, and there would spring from behind its walls a reception delegation, holding red flags and looking as official as it could in its somewhat indeterminate clothing. Sometimes we stopped briefly for these people, and there was some hand-shaking, coffee-drinking and exchanging of sentiments; but the Sultan was in a hurry, and sometimes we did little more than wave at them, leaving them (oddly enough) anything but crest-fallen, but more often roaring with laughter and congratulating each other. A few solitary camel-men passed by, sometimes riding in a peculiar kneeling position behind the hump, and it was strange to see with what totally unmoved calm these men and their animals received the appearance of our convoy, now bigger, bolder and brassier than ever. Once, in this difficult semi-desert country, all bumps and scrubs, the steering on one of the Sultan's trucks went wrong, and the thing went skidding dizzily over the track. We abandoned it, the qadi, who was riding in the front, cheerfully transferring himself to another; but within a few miles we found, miraculously deposited beside the track, the wreck of another identical truck left there earlier by the field force or the oil company. Its steering gear proved to be undamaged, and it was quickly cannibalized. In an hour or two our convoy was complete again. 'God is always merciful to the traveller,' said the Sultan when I mentioned the incident to him later.

Miles, writing about Ibri in 1910, remarked feelingly: 'The tribes occupying it are one and all thieving, treacherous and turbulent. The quantity of available rascaldom is pretty considerable, and the quality of ruffianism is quite in keeping.' So it was a surprise to me, when we eventually approached this place of ill-repute, to find that it looked the most peaceful, serene and inviting of all the Omani towns. A white hill rose above it to the east; a vegetated plain stretched away to the south; and Ibri lay sheltered in fresh groves of fruit and palm trees, like an egg in a green nest. Two big fallujes ran down from the hillside, and though the buildings of the place were dusty and derelict, its setting was delectably lush.

When I wandered into the town that afternoon I found it to be a place of very marked character. The Sultan was to meet the assembled leaders that evening, in the main square of the town, so I occupied the intervening hours by loitering through its streets and alley-ways. It was the archetype of the Arabian oasis town idealized by so many poets and depicted by so many slushy artists. A narrow walled lane led between orchards to the centre of Ibri. It was cool and shady, its infrequent patches of sunshine speckled by the shadows of the branches above. There was a soft, liquid, soothing mystery to this sequestered alley, almost velvety in flavour; I padded along its soft sandy surface with my eyes half closed, as in a dream. Old stone walls lined it, and a little stream ran beside it, and now and then crooked wooden gateways led into the neighbouring orchards. I peered through the cracks in one such gate, guarded by a smiling dog with its ears cut off (to improve its hearing) and saw into the rich orchards beyond: mangoes, limes, apricots, figs, bananas, pomegranates, peaches, quinces, oranges, plums, melons, and squashy Arabian fruits whose names I could not even guess at. The shafts of sunlight were opaque with slow-moving dust, but the trees were green and solemn, like forests of little redwoods.

I passed a few black-robed housewives on the way, and presently the path debouched into a small square, in the centre of which a flight of steps led down to the falluj. Crowds of women thronged this place, and from the pit there were vibrant wailing sounds. A few men lingered on the outskirts, toying with their canes; but the throng was predominantly female, and most of the women wore fearsome peaked black masks, stiff and hot-looking, related to the ones I had seen on Arab ladies in Dhufar. The cumulative effect of sixty or seventy women disfigured by these things was horrifying; with their black hanging robes, their dirty hands, their screeching voices and their beaked concealed faces, they were like huge hungry birds of prey hovering around carrion. I made my way through the crowd to the top of the steps, and looked down them to the water below; and there at the bottom three or four masked women were bathing the small emaciated body of a child, while their companions on the stone-flagged platform moaned distressfully. The steps were crowded to suffocation, and the stench was unpleasant: but the women took no notice of me at all, and I stood there for a moment watching, chilled by the scene.

A hand touched my shoulder, and a voice said in English: 'Good morning, mister! You shouldn't stand about here, you know, you might catch something! The sanitation is ever so bad!' It was the proselyte who had translated for me, with such appealing missionary conviction, the Sultan's speech to his soldiers. To my astonishment he was dressed from head to foot in a long white pall-like garment, and over his arm he carried a towel: with his gaunt face and large eyes he looked like the celebrated picture Dr. Donne had painted of himself standing in his shroud, and his appearance at that particular moment gave me quite a start. His bearing was much more spectral than military, and his conversation, too, inclined to the melancholy.

He had, however, nothing to do with the rites at the falluj, for he took my arm and hastened me away. He had been bathing, he said, and would be pleased if I would now come and visit the house he had taken in Ibri. It was a mistake to hang about the falluj too much, for the sanitary arrangements were something shocking, not at all like what he had been accustomed to at the mission. 'You never saw such funny people as these, mister. I daren't tell them I'm a Christian.

91

They would kill me! Though I must say', he added with a disarming smile, 'I married ever such a nice Muslim girl. What else could I do? There wasn't a Christian girl to be found in the whole of Muscat and Oman!'

Chuckling as we walked, for the idea of his concealed faith seemed to amuse him, and something piquant about his personality certainly pleased me, we made our way leisurely to his house. It lay behind a heavy gate (there was ever such bad robbers in Ibri, said the soldier) and was surrounded by a cool garden. As we entered the door of the house I saw, half hidden in a dim and smoky recess, four or five black shrouded figures, almost motionless, and soundless but for a few low moaning noises. A small fire burnt through the murk of this dismal alcove, and sometimes there was a swishing sound, as of the movement of very old and extremely dirty draperies. I did not like to ask what was happening in there, thinking that perhaps some acolytes of the soldier's were performing clandestine Christian ceremonies, like saints in catacombs: but as we climbed the staircase he remarked casually, hitching up his shroud: 'That's my wife. She's got something wrong with her inside, so a few friends came in to look after her.' I could scarcely imagine a more unpromising form of treatment, so sepulchral was the atmosphere of that cave-like place, but the husband seemed perfectly happy about it, and we sat pleasantly in an upstairs room, watching the passers-by from a window and eating some rather stringy pomegranates. Yes, he sighed, Ibri was a funny place. The people was very funny. Their behaviour was ever so queer. You never knew what they would do next. Very ignorant they was, and very dirty, and the sanitation was ever so bad. 'It's awful, really,' concluded the apostate, removing a pip from between his two front teeth.

I maundered on into the town, and found it in a state of high expectancy. Hundreds of sheikhs and their followers had gathered in the main square, beside the sequence of crumbled walls called the fort (it had never recovered from a nineteenth-century earthquake); and a jolly lot they proved to be. I had been told that, despite the traditional puritanism of Ibri and the rigid tenets of the Imamate, a good deal of date wine was made in the town; and certainly some of these merry old boys seemed to have found themselves a drink somewhere. Moreover, despite the ban on tobacco—in theory even more firmly enforced by the Imam than by the Sultan—everybody smoked small wooden pipes, using tobacco with a tangy, bitter smell to it, not at all disagreeable. I met nothing but friendliness in Ibri. In the suk, a busy, well-stocked market (razor-blades, English soap-flakes, gay Indian textiles) I found the shop-keepers and idlers curious but helpful, and as I wandered through the streets I collected a little train of well-wishers, a motley shabby crew, who indefatigably pointed out the wonders of that small metropolis (and many of them, indeed, I might otherwise have overlooked). I noticed that the shopfronts were secured with padlocks of monumental size, but all these attendant citizens seemed, for Arabia, unusually frank and straightforward. We stopped for ten minutes to watch a goldsmith at work in his dim-lit open-fronted shop. He appeared to be a Persian, for he was wearing a costume (high-crowned hat, tight-sleeved jerkin, sandals and odd appendages) that reminded me of some of the craftsmen in the bazaars of Isfahan and Teheran; and in his eye there was a look, like the look in the eye of a particularly experienced and humorous lizard, that seemed to show he had mastered the old Persian techniques of human relations. He paid no attention to me at all, except that when we left him, still hammering at tiny pieces of metal with infinitesimal implements, he raised one dark hooded eye and gave me the faintest insidious suspicion of a wink.

Elsewhere we paused to talk to a group of young bucks standing in a side-street. They suggested I might like to meet the sheikh of their community, who was at that moment preparing himself to face the Sultan. We walked down the lane and into a mud house with a good wooden door, and there was the old sheikh, a handsome figure, sitting all alone on the floor.

He did not seem to be preparing himself very actively: indeed, further preparation would be difficult, for he was embellished with every kind of finery, and was almost as highly scented as the ruler. This old dandy was not at all surprised to see me, but at once motioned to me to sit down and called for coffee. 'A happy day,' he remarked unctuously, probably supposing I was some official caller. 'The Sultan in Ibri! I never thought I would live to see it. The wicked Imam gone, and the Sultan of Oman here amongst us. Thanks be to God!' I thought I heard a stifled giggle from one of the young men, but when the sheikh and I both turned around to see, their faces were as solemn as sphinxes.

The same underlying levity of approach to grave matters was also apparent in the square, where the Arabs, armed to the teeth, were waiting for the Sultan in a mood of holiday. Now and then some gay spirit would loose off a rifle magazine into the air, raising the question (in my mind, if in nobody else's) whether what goes up must not eventually come down again. My companions admitted that at these events somebody did occasionally get hurt, but seemed fairly confident that it would never be them; and nobody in the entire assembly moved an inch or even jumped when such a salvo rang out within a few feet of their ears. On the contrary, they all sat there very comfortably, sipping coffee and smoking their pipes. A group of formidable laughing men was pointed out to me as sheikhs of the Duru, the paramount tribe of that region, who alone knew the route into the quicksand we had passed on our way to Fahud, and who also operated a salt mine presented to them by the Sultan's father. They were powerful men with a look of determined independence, well in accord with their tribe's reputation for the total disregard of outside authority. The Duru, who owned large herds of excellent camels, were blood-enemies of our friends the Yal Wahabis, but for the moment their perennial hostilities seemed, mercifully, to be silenced.

I joined a group of tribesmen sitting in a circle on the ground. 'How old do you think my rifle is?' asked one of them.

This was an embarrassing question, for the weapon looked to me Cromwellian; its fittings were elaborate and ornate, and many years before its barrel had evidently been split in an excess of ferocity, for it seemed to be spliced together with wire.

'Let me see,' said I, examining it closely while I wondered what to say, 'I should think—well, now—I should say twenty, twenty-five years old?'

Gusts of derisive laughter greeted this careful reply. The owner of the rifle looked around at his audience as if he had produced an unusually pink rabbit out of a hat. The young men clapped their hands, and the old ones laughed so heartily that some of them were seized with fits of painful coughing.

'This rifle', said the owner to me, 'belonged to my father's father's father. It's eighty-three years old. The oldest rifle in Ibri. And another thing,' added this man, who evidently enjoyed a reputation as a wit, 'how much do you pay for a wife in England?'

But before I had time to answer he leapt agilely to his feet, and grasping my arm led me down a narrow pathway off the square. Soon he was knocking at the door of an outstandingly dirty and ramshackle house. It opened at once, and there stood in the doorway a small smiling negress with dangling ear-rings. Her dress was sombre—a long black gown and a sort of dingy turban—but her face was unveiled and lavishly painted with henna, and there was something about her deportment so incorrigibly eager and amoral that I nearly turned and ran. The Arab, however, seized her hand with a few words of lewd endearment and stood to face me. 'Here,' said he, 'take our photo!'

But I had no time, for at that moment there was one of the excruciating cannon-blasts that always foretold the arrival of the Sultan. The clown and I ran back to the square, looking behind us at the corner to see the negress waving us an exceedingly coy and suggestive good-bye. There was no sign of the Sultan, but the more important of the sheikhs had ranged themselves in a vast rectangle, in which they stood meditatively, like minor canons, sometimes raising their rifles into the air for a sporadic *feu de joie*. In the corner of the square, beneath the fort, stood the big gun. It had no carriage, and its barrel was propped upon a log. The gunners were having a splendid time ramming gunpowder into its muzzle with poles, firing the fuse, and then scampering away like urchins before the bang came. Most of the company was totally unmoved by the explosions; but the gunners seemed to think that though it was all great fun it might be wise to keep well away from the cannon.

When the Sultan swept up in his truck, he led all the waiting sages into a kind of shack made of carpets, of a sort commonly used in the Arab countries for funeral celebrations. Carpets, a little threadbare, lined the floor; and carpets, rather faded, were elevated on sticks to form the roofs and walls. There was only one entrance, and the inside was therefore shaded, lit only by the sunshine that crept in through the door and the corners. It was like the sham tents that English children used to erect in gardens on August afternoons, using tarpaulins and eiderdowns.

I peered in through the door, and saw the Sultan sitting in misty majesty at the far end of the tent, where the illumination was dimmest. One or two functionaries sat near him, their legs tucked under them. The rest of the assembly had settled down in two long rows, one on each side, holding sticks and rifles. As I watched, a slave came hastening over to me. The Sultan had noticed me, standing inquisitively there, and invited me to join the session. This was awkward. It was the Arab custom to remove one's shoes at such an occasion, and I knew that I had some ugly holes in my socks: still, I could scarcely refuse, so I kicked my shoes off and walked across the carpet trying to tuck my toes under the soles of my feet, in a manner which might have looked odd to a company more accustomed to Europeans, but which did not seem to raise many eyebrows there.

I had been to functions of this character before, but had almost forgotten the appalling boredom of them. The Sultan sat silently wearing his autocratic look and the coffee-pourers padded up and down, and a man with a bowl offered us a huge mass of sweet sticky stuff like calf's-foot jelly: but nobody said a word. The Arabs sat there stiff as statues, only moving to finger their beards or adjust their robes, sometimes twiddling their canes or shifting their rifles, but never smiling, whispering, expectorating or even coughing. They would have made an admirable concert audience, but I soon began to wish some irrepressible rebel would raise a cry of sedition, or at least that my friend the dandy (who sat self-consciously very near the Sultan) would kiss the ruler's sandalled foot. But the Arab is intensely conscious of the proprieties, and not a word was uttered nor a single indiscretion committed. When the Sultan rose to his feet, with an eagle-like glance around the tent, the Arabs all rose too and followed him into the sunshine. It was like moving from one world to another to leave that hall of protocol and rejoin the jokers outside, still smoking their pipes in the dust. (The Sultan later decreed that, since smoking seemed to be so deep-rooted a habit in Ibri, it might continue in private: but public expression of the vice must cease.)

If Nizwa might be said to be the Mecca of our journey, and Ibri perhaps its Reno or Monte Carlo, Buraimi can best be likened to Yalta; for there the Sultan was to meet the Sheikh of Abu Dhabi to set the stamp of ceremonial upon their amicable divisions of influence. Even the small-scale map I carried with me showed clearly why this remote oasis had for so long been a key to the control of south-east Arabia. It stood on the very edge of the sand desert, in a crucial position at the base of the Oman peninsula. Five main caravan routes were marked on my map, and all of them passed through Buraimi, for it was the only big watering-place in the area. It commanded the easiest route across the hills to the sea; the route to Nizwa and the interior of Oman; and the routes from the Arabian hinterland to the sheikhdoms of the Trucial Coast. Because of this strategic situation it had long been a centre of the slave trade, in which negroes from Zanzibar or Africa were conveyed to the customers of interior Arabia; and it had been the Saudi gateway, for arms and influence, to Oman and the Gulf sheikhdoms. Buraimi was really a group of nine villages, and the Saudis claimed them all on historical grounds. The British view was that six of the villages legally belonged to Abu Dhabi and three to the Sultan (and in this opinion the two potentates cordially concurred). The legal position was distinctly obscure. The lawyers of the American oil company in Saudi Arabia were said to believe in all honesty that sovereignty should be Saudi; so did, I was assured, at least one British Orientalist of international repute; and the matter had actually gone for international arbitration at Geneva. The Saudis, however, had spoiled their own case by resorting to methods of overt bribery, perfectly acceptable in Arabia and employed by all parties, but damning in the sphere of international law. An excellent excuse had therefore been presented for the expulsion of the Saudi forces from the oasis. The strong British action of a few months before had so far provoked only angry squeals from Riyad and Cairo, and the Sheikh and the Sultan were now converging upon the place as Stalin and his peers converged so fatefully upon the rococo hotel at Yalta.

The odd thing about Buraimi, once we got there, was its curiously nebulous character. We drove through pleasant country to reach it, with the mountains standing invitingly to the east; and passed a number of date groves and forts; and saw a few Arabs assembled outside a few huts, with four statuesque figures cramming charges into a black cannon; and all of a sudden we realized that this was the heart of Buraimi, and the shapeless settlements that bounded our horizon were the famous nine villages of the oasis. There seemed to be no obvious centre, crux or centrifugal force to guide us in our wandering. One end of Buraimi was some miles from the other, and the palm groves and mud houses straggled untidily over the countryside. No doubt if we had been struggling with a team of refractory camels across the limitless desert this place might have seemed a little Paradise, but I was disappointed with this lack of substance or cohesion. The touch-points of modern power struggles, from Fashoda to the 38th Parallel, have seldom been beauty spots.

I walked about the oasis for a time and, though I saw no shackled slaves or sealed crates of munitions, did come across one small piece of evidence that the Saudi bribe-masters had been active in Buraimi. I sat down for coffee with a group of friendly and eager tribesmen, and one of them, looking as if he had lived all his life on the back of a camel, suddenly reached across and grabbed my wrist. He wanted to see my watch, he said. Was it a Longines? I understood this well-informed interest, for I knew it was the practice of the Saudis to distribute gift watches according to makes: the more important the recipient, the more distinguished the watchmaker. Thus, since the cases were almost always gold, the best way to size up a man's significance to the Saudi cause was to discover the maker's name, and many a poor politician or journalist, returning from a visit to Riyad, had flourished his handsome present from the court without knowing how surely it stamped his status in the Arab world. My Arabs looked a little baffled, for my watch was made by a firm not patronized by the royal house, so that I might have been either desperately important or not worth a second thought. They did not seem to care much, anyway, but showed me their own watches, set by the sun (as is the custom in those Arab countries) and told me with satisfaction that mine was seven hours slow.

There had been an assembling of dignitaries at Buraimi, of a different sort from those provincial gatherings that had greeted us hitherto. At Buraimi our small ambitions were synthesized with greater issues—cold wars, the struggles of economic giants, the fortunes of empires, the accounts of companies. The British Raj was therefore represented here, in the person of a witty and astringent political officer and the charming political agent from Dubai, on the coast. The British War Office, too, which had played its part in all our affairs, had its representatives: Buraimi had been occupied by troops of the Trucial Oman Levies (nothing to do with the Sultan) which were led by regular British Army officers. The youngest brother of the Sheikh of Abu Dhabi—the man who had, so it was reported, refused a bribe of £20 m. to desert to the Saudis—was in attendance as his brother's representative in the oasis: he was an intelligent and personable man who had, unlike many Arabs of his kind, a ready sympathy for Bedouin tastes and customs. There was thus a cosmopolitan and sophisticated air to the company which greeted us in Buraimi, far removed from the goat's-hair, grass-roots flavour of previous receptions. Our camp was pitched on Abu Dhabi soil, either by mistake or as a gesture of solidarity, and we settled down that night to await the arrival of Shakhbut bin Sultan, the celebrated Sheikh of that territory.

I had heard a great deal about this man in the course of my travels in the Middle East. His sheikhdom, often at odds with its neighbours in the manner of the Trucial Coast, had not yet been blessed with oil; but he was a person of an inquiring turn of mind, adaptable and receptive, and eager almost to the point of eccentricity. A friend of mine once described a journey he had made with Shakhbut across part of his sheikhdom. I asked him what the sheikh had talked about in the course of the several hours they spent together. He replied that the conversation had ranged over a very wide variety of subjects, but that he only remembered two specific questions put by the ruler. The first was: did my friend think it possible that man would soon devise a means of reaching the moon? The second was: according to my friend's latest information, what was the proportion of Protestants to Catholics in the city of Hamburg? The inquiries may be apocryphal; but they are, I am sure, genuinely illustrative of Shakhbut's unusual mind and avidity for all sorts of knowledge.

He certainly had a taste for modernity rather more spectacular than the Sultan's restrained yearnings in that direction, for he arrived next morning along the track from his capital in an enormous Cadillac convertible of flaming yellow, from the windows of which his humorous face, with bushy eyebrows and a sensual mouth, looked out at us appraisingly. He was wearing the usual sumptuous clothes, and stepped from the car in that lordly Arab manner that sometimes hovers on the fringes of caricature; but he looked to me like a man unusually well able to look after himself. He probably inherited some instinct for self-preservation, for the history of his dynasty had been exceptionally violent, even for Arabia. There had been fourteen ruling sheikhs before Shakhbut. Eight of these had been murdered (four of them by the agency of their own brothers); four had been deposed or expelled (one by his brother, one by his son); and only two had died peacefully in their sheikhly beds at Abu Dhabi. Within the past few years a number of Shakbut's nearest relatives had deserted him for the Saudi cause, and at one time planned an invasion of his territory, financed by Saudi gold. No wonder there was a certain wariness in his eye, and a hungry search for truth evident in his conversation.

There stepped from the car behind him a tall Englishman carrying a camera, who introduced himself to me as the sheikh's Court Poet. This agreeable person was, in fact, an author who was writing a book about the Persian Gulf and who was Shakhbut's guest on this expedition rather as I was the Sultan's. He seemed to be enjoying himself greatly, and the Sheikh appeared to view his presence with pride, perhaps remembering, in truth, the days when such great Arab chieftains had their own poets and ballad-mongers to inspire them in battle and record their moments of splendour.

Behind the poet came two rugged retainers, of leathery skin, carrying on their wrists a pair of hooded falcons; the sheikh was to combine this gesture of statesmanship with a hunting trip in the desert. The falcons looked like those noble god-birds portrayed in the art of the ancient Egyptians, so still and proud did they sit upon their masters' wrists or, later, upon the carved wooden perches that were stuck in the sand for them. One of

them, of surpassing hauteur, was pointed out to me as a famous
hunter, a man-of-war among peregrines, worth a substantial
sum of money (for falconing was the chief winter pastime of the
rich Persian Gulf sheikhs). Such birds were caught on the
islands of the Trucial Coast, by what sounded to me alarming
methods. The trapper concealed himself in a pit covered with
scrub; he then tied a stone to the leg of a pigeon and allowed
the bird to flutter in the air until it attracted the attention of a
falcon. When the hawk had killed the pigeon it was unable to
fly away with it, because of the weight of the stone, so it later
returned to the spot to make a meal of it there. The trapper,
having moved the pigeon as near as possible to the pit, then
awaited his moment tensely; until, at the moment of crisis, he
was able to reach out a hand from beneath the scrub and grasp
the falcon by its powerful leg. Looking at Shakhbut's ferocious
peregrines, I did not much like the sound of this task; but I was
assured that a real affection was often established betwen bird
and master, once the shock of the first meeting had been
forgotten.

A traditional bard would certainly have woven a poem about
our celebratory breakfast the next day. Sultan and Sheikh had
their meeting, discussed their policies, congratulated each
other on their successes, and generally agreed about things:
and there followed an immense and memorable banquet, to
which on the following morning we all made our way across the
soft Buraimi sand. A tent had been erected for the occasion, of
considerable size, but the banquet was much too big for it, and
the food stretched away on its runners far beyond the confines
of the marquee. I cannot begin to describe the profusion of it
all. There were huge camel haunches, of course, stuffed with
spices and other meats; platters of obscure and sickly sweet
things; great slabs of mutton; unfamiliar savouries of all
descriptions, and a plethora of the more usual Oriental
stalwarts; mountains of rice; and two plates, strategically
disposed, of succulent bustard. The guests ranged themselves

on the ground about this splendid buffet, the Sultan and the Sheikh at the head, the rest of us packed tightly around the sides. The qadi blessed our food in his beguiling, quavering voice; and the banquet began.

I would not say that it was a comfortable meal, for the decrees of Arab etiquette were so rigid, the company so exalted, the occasion so memorable, and the desire of everybody present to do the right thing so intense, that very few of us got anything to eat at all. In the first place you might only eat at such events with your right hand, and this rather limited your field of action in an arena as wide as this; in the second place everybody thought it wise to keep an eye on the two rulers, to follow their unimpeachable example; and in the third place the two rulers were no less inhibited than anyone else; so that we sat there hamstrung, hardly daring to speak. Sometimes somebody grabbed a handful of rice and squeezed it between his fingers, to remove the grease, with a slight but perceptible squelching noise. Sometimes some rash spirit made an attack on a camel haunch, only to find that the particular piece he coveted was so firmly affixed to the rest of the meat that he had to embark upon an appallingly embarrassing struggle with sinews, bones and stuffing before he could detach any of it. The bustard, *pièce de résistance* of the feast, had been planted so firmly in the middle of the table that it was virtually impossible to reach it, and it remained there in a condition of complacent virginity.

Only an occasional diffident murmur enlivened the echoing silence of the tent, though I dare say that at the bottom end of the banquet, well away from the ears of potentates, things went a little more amusingly. An English major sitting on my left occasionally allowed himself a tart irreverence, and the wali, sitting primly on the other side, sometimes uttered something pious. The Court Poet, who had a camera with him, asked the Sultan and Shakhbut if he might take their photographs. The Sultan said yes, provided he did not do it while he was eating rice, because the stuff would run down his chin so. The political officer also took a photograph, with a very small German camera. The Sultan said what a nice exposure meter. I said it wasn't an exposure meter, it was a German camera especially made for spies. The Sultan said: 'I see.'

So we toyed with that marvellous spread for an hour or so, making no appreciable dents in it, until the two rulers, smiling at each other sententiously, led the rest of us out of the tent. A huge crowd of onlookers—camel-men, soldiers, villagers, slaves—had gathered on the ridge above the marquee and stood there poised, like a wave at the turn of its crest, as we walked slowly towards the camp. As soon as the Sultan and the Sheikh were out of sight, and were shaking hands ceremonially, that vast tattered army leapt off the sand-dunes and fell on the food like ants, not desisting until every scrap of it had gone, camels and sweetmeats and rice and all; and somebody even trod across the table-cloth to rape the bustard.

7

*Across the mountains—Wadi Jeziz—coal—Sohar
—the sea—on Sindbad—mercenaries—naval calls
—down the sands—bats*

Our departure from Buraimi was dramatic, for as our big
convoy assembled, warmed its engines, and moved off towards
the hills, the Sheikh of Abu Dhabi roared alongside us in his
yellow Cadillac. For a while he escorted us (off his territory, as
it happened, but more like a destroyer than a game-keeper)
and I could see his long swarthy face through the open window
of his car, rising and falling with the swell of the ground. Our
Yalta had apparently been a success. At least it was remarkable
to see two potent Arab leaders, in a part of the world so
notorious for implacable feuds and jealousies, agreeing
amicably to the division of a crucial oasis. The immediate
future of the place seemed to be settled; and when the big
convertible wheeled about to return to the oasis, the Court Poet
(sitting in the back seat) waved good-bye to me and Shakhbut
intimated a courtly *bon voyage* to the Sultan.

We planned to reach Sohar, on the gulf of Oman, that
evening, making due allowance for those several ceremonies of
welcome and obeisance with which the villagers were sure to
delay our progress. Accordingly we drove swiftly out of the

plain, soon leaving the scattered groves of Buraimi far out of sight, and made for the only possible pass through the mountains, called the Wadi Jeziz. (Above Nizwa another ravine crossed to Muscat—a journey of about ninety miles, instead of the 500 we were now undertaking—and this would be passable if a jumble of big boulders at its summit could be cleared. The oil company was planning to put a road through this pass to connect Fahud directly with the Gulf of Oman, revolutionizing communications within south-east Arabia; and the Sultan, who was planning a return overland journey to Dhufar, hoped to be able to use it on the way home.)

So we plunged into the hills merrily and unerringly, like horses scenting the stables. The last part of our odyssey had begun, and in three days we would be in Muscat. The wadi was quite unlike any other country we had crossed. It was a narrow winding pass between bleak hills, reminding me often of the highlands of Edom in southern Jordan, in the heart of which the Nabateans built Petra; but at convenient intervals it was lavishly watered by springs, and so our journey became a patchwork of the green and the arid. Delectable oases had sprung up around these springs and thrived on the associated fallujes. You could hardly see the buildings for the trees, except that sometimes the big brooding tower of a fort protruded above the palms or loomed between the trunks; the greenery was so generous that it often flowed over the surrounding walls, creating patches of shade on our dusty track. Sometimes such cool places were also blessed with a shallow pool, with an Arab boy reflected in it, or a knot of women clustered at its edge to watch us go by; and these often gave the scene a Constablian air, so that you expected to see Salisbury spire rising among the hills, or hear the jingling of harness brasses. Fruits and vegetables of many kinds grew in these inviting settlements, and the people seemed to be uncommonly skilful in cultivating such fundamentally unpromising land; impressive to see, when you remembered that for countless generations their principal occupation had been annihilating one another. Moreover, they

seemed on the whole more cheerful and healthy than any of the
other Omanis we had met. I remember in particular one very
small but fat boy, wearing a short robe with a ragged hem,
dancing with excitement to see us pass, more like a figure from
Dickens than a child from Arabia. Two laughing old men, of
similarly Christmassy flavour, were restraining him from
behind; and this little tableau of three, all rather rotund, was
silhouetted against the black open doorway of a house, etching
it very distinctly on my memory.

Once, in a narrow defile, we passed through a section of rock
that looked to me unmistakably like coal—known to exist in
these highlands, but never exploited. The convoy stopped suddenly, and I saw that a slave had jumped off the Sultan's truck
and was prising a lump of the stuff away from the rock. The
Sultan was 'very interested in these things'. Later, I believe, a
fuller geological survey was undertaken; but at that time the
only knowledge of these mountains had been gleaned by explorers working in extremely difficult and dangerous
conditions many years before. There was certainly coal, and no
less certainly iron—the Nizwa iron-masters used to work upon
ore extracted locally, and there were still plenty of traces of it.
Oil we all hoped for; and I was so struck, once or twice, by
resemblances between this country and the Colorado Plateau,
on the other side of the world, that I wondered if the Sultanate
might not be harbouring deposits of uranium. Anyway, the
chunk of coal was thrown into the truck; the Sultan made a
careful note of it in his diary; and away we went. Nothing
impressed upon me more forcibly the extraordinarily remote
and shuttered nature of Oman than this ignorance about what
the place was even made of. The wheel-ruts in our track, made
by the soldiers on their way to Buraimi, were evidence that at
last this closeted corner was being opened to the world; but
until now it had been like a populated Atlantis, an island of
hearsay between the desert and the sea. All the great empires of
the world had recognized the importance of the Persian Gulf.
Alexander had sent his fleets into it. French, British and Dutch

had vied for supremacy over it. Peter the Great, in his alleged will, urged his successors to dominate it. Imperial Germany pressed towards it. The early Russian Communists saw it as a principal prize of their power-drive. Yet Oman, commanding the entrance to the Gulf, remained less familiar than Tibet or Greenland.

Our way rose sharply, through well-populated country, past strings of villages with agreeable names. We had not followed the shortest route up the wadi, for there were one or two gatherings of well-wishers, off the main track, whose sentiments the Sultan thought it worth while to cultivate. Nevertheless, by the middle of the afternoon we found ourselves on the ridge of the hills at about 2,000 feet. Here we apparently passed from the jurisdiction of one of the Sultan's private armies to that of another, rather as in America you suddenly find yourself confronted by state police in totally unfamiliar uniforms, enforcing altogether unsuspected laws. At the top of the pass there was a small guard post, manned by a platoon of soldiers of rather more ceremonial bearing than the field force we had left behind. These were troops of the Batinah Force, which had fought the battle against the fugitive Talib. They presented arms with extreme smartness and were briefly inspected by the Sultan; the cloud of blanco that arose from their webbing, the clang of their rifles and the precise clatter of their boots summoned all kinds of nostalgic associations for me, strangely incongruous in that setting (like the officer cadets at Katmandu, who march to graduation to the strains of *Auld Lang Syne*).

Soon we could see in the distance the blue line of the sea, and a perceptible thrill ran through our heterogeneous company. There is always something miraculous about fulfilling geography. We had crossed (just as the maps said we would) from the Arabian Sea to the Gulf of Oman, clean across the triangle of south-east Arabia; and we had proved that a stout truck with a resolute driver could travel across Arabia from one side to another, from Aden to Muscat, 1,500 miles without an inch of tarmac. Down the hillside we went uproariously, the slaves exhilarated by the prospect ahead of them, my driver recklessly overjoyed. There was a stretch of dry country to cross, sterile and unadorned, and then we found ourselves summarily among the tremendous palm groves of the Batinah coast, mile upon mile of tall fertility, millions of trees, thousands of green acres, in one of the richest date-growing regions on earth. The paths between these trees were intolerably dusty, so that our wheels sank into the dust and thick clouds of it obscured the way and dirtied all our possessions; but there was something fine and awe-inspiring about so vast a garden of palms, suddenly standing there beneath the mountains. When we passed a big camel caravan, its bags bulging with dates, lurching heavily to Muscat, I remembered Mohammed's legendary injunction: 'Honour your aunt, the palm, which was made of the same clay as Adam.'

On the edge of these groves, in the narrow sandy space between the palm trees and the sea, stood the town of Sohar, dominated by the usual fort (facing the ocean) but surrounded by thousands of straggling palm-frond houses, all along the beach. This was a place of significance for the Sultan. The founder of his sultanly dynasty had been the Governor of Sohar in 1744, at the time when, in a brilliant *coup d'état*, he had taken advantage of the prevailing confused situation to become master of Muscat and Oman. (In those days the ruler was called the Imam of Oman: the sultanship, and the establishment of Muscat as a capital, came later.) Nevertheless, when we jumped out of our trucks on the beach, and the slaves pitched our tents on the very brink of the surf, it was not of these historical antecedents that the Sultan spoke to me. 'The last time I was here', said he, 'was in 1952 when all the tribes had assembled here to march with me upon Buraimi. It was a very interesting sight, so many tribesmen, you know, all with their camels on the beach. At that time, as you may have heard, the British prevented me from moving on Buraimi, but the tribesmen were quite prepared for it. I hope you are still comfortable, Mr. Morris,' he added politely, 'not too tired, I hope?'

Later I was given a description, more detailed but perhaps less heartfelt than the Sultan's, of the tribes gathering on the beach at Sohar to march over the mountains and expel the Saudis from Buraimi: thousands of them massed there beside the sea, flamboyant individualists and patient followers, with their multitudes of animals, their colours and their bright weapons. 'We couldn't let them do it,' a British diplomatist told me later still. 'The Americans were so mixed up in it all. When the Saudis moved into Buraimi they even travelled in American transport. Suppose the Sultan had gone in under our auspices, and some idiotic American geologist had got himself killed! There'd have been hell to pay. It just wasn't worth the risk then.'

'What did the Sultan say, when he heard he couldn't go ahead with it?'

'I wasn't there to hear, but I imagine—what d'you think?— I imagine he just said: "I see." '

It was a heavenly beach we found ourselves upon. The sand was crisp and even, and littered with queer sea-shells. In its upper reaches, where the sand petered away into the soil, it was also patterned with the mesh-work of innumerable little marrow-like plants, intricate and delicate, like veins in the ground. This vegetable was unpleasant to eat, I was told, but was useful both as a medicine and as an aphrodisiac. I wandered far down the beach that evening, past the strings of burastis, and looked at the footprints of sea-birds in the soft sand. It was odd to be transported in this way, across a desert and two mountain ranges, to a quite different sea; and to realize that not so far away across the water stood Persia and the frontiers of Pakistan, when a few days before I had been in the bosom of continental Arabia.

A mile or so up the beach I came across a small fresh-water pool, swarming with fish. Cranes stood impassively upon its bank, and the tall palm trees were reflected in its surface precisely as upon the lids of chocolate boxes. A middle-aged man was washing his feet in the water, and I sat down beside him, trying to ignore the smell of mud and decay that arose disconcertingly from the pool. What kind of a place was Sohar? I asked him. Nothing much now, he said, but it had been a great city once, the greatest on this coastline, rich and powerful. (It had, indeed, enjoyed its times of independence; when d'Albuquerque captured it in 1507 its garrison included more than fifty knights clad in steel armour, with the forequarters of their horses also plated.) What was more, said my informant, rubbing his feet with the bottom of his gown, Sohar was the birthplace of Sindbad the Sailor.

People often said this to me during our stay in Muscat and Oman, but I cannot believe it to have much substance in fact or even, for that matter, in myth. The *Arabian Nights*—which have Indian, Persian and even perhaps Greek ancestries—seem to make it plain that Sindbad was a Baghdadi, who began his disastrous voyages from Basra; and nearly all of his adventures seem, by the nature of things, to have befallen him upon islands. Whenever the captain cried: 'My masters, all is lost!' there was always an island within reach for Sindbad: but the only reference to a coast-line that could possibly be the Batinah comes when the captain, referring to his magic book, remarks that the land to be seen upon the horizon is the Clime of Kings, 'inhabited by monsters and terrible serpents'.

However, as we sat there talking beside the pool I was suddenly reminded of the Old Man of the Sea, sitting beside *his* pool in his great cloak made of leaves; and taking another look at my companion, whose form was dissolving creepily in the dusk, I wished him good night and left him hastily. The camp was all in darkness when I returned to it, and there was a gentle murmur of surf upon the sand. The full moon came up so huge and pale that for a few moments I thought it was some great white ship sailing by; but no ships sailed near the Batinah coast, except the little white fishing boats of the Muscatis, and

111

no well-heeled Baghdadi merchants had been washed up for years.

The headquarters of the Batinah Force was at Sohar, in a delightful white house beside the sea, built by a member of the ruling family. A parade was mounted for the Sultan, very smart and conscientious, and only deficient in music, for a band had not yet been formed. There was a shooting display, too. This interested the Sultan more, for though he had little taste for military matters, and always looked more dutiful than cheerful at these parades, he was a keen marksman; so keen that on the wall beside the sea at Dhufar there stood a row of bottles, at which the ruler, in any idle moment, would take pot-shots with a rifle from the window of his palace. The military cantonment at Sohar was scrupulously clean and well-kept, with bright red doors and brass padlocks, reminiscent of mews houses in Chelsea.

Two British officers ran this little army, and I enjoyed talking to them as some of the last of the British mercenaries among the Arabs. It had been many a long year since the Arab Revolt, when the British military connection with the Arabs had been so dashingly founded. Forty years had passed since Captain Shakespear, Ibn Saud's 'finest Englishman', had been killed fighting with the Wahabis against Ibn Rashid. The memory of Lawrence had long since faded (Burton and Doughty were often remembered more clearly) and the roar of those old Rolls-Royce armoured cars was silenced even in recollection. The Druze Legion was only a legend. The Iraq Levies had been dispersed. The military mission at Riyad had been told its services were no longer required. Within a few months Glubb Pasha would be dismissed from the Arab Legion, and the British elements of that gorgeous force would be whittled away. Soon it would only be in a few remote corners of the Arabian Peninsula that Englishmen could still serve as soldiers with Arabs, relishing the particular pleasure that stems from living with desert people in conditions of shared hardship. Many of the remaining mercenaries were former officers of the Indian Army. Those with the field force had served with a famous irregular regiment called the South Waziristan Scouts, and were well used to free-thinking, independent tribal soldiers; others (like many ex-Indian civil servants) were not so successful in their dealings with Arabs, expecting from them too unquestioning a sense of discipline and respect, forgetting that to the average Arab every man is as good as his brother, and must be asked to do things nicely.

It was a sad concomitant of fading Empire that such openings for soldierly adventures abroad were getting fewer every year; for by a happy paradox nothing had done more to increase amity among peoples. Gone now was the old Indian Army, and all those brave gallivantings in the Indian hills. Gone were the African wars, and the gunboats on the Yangtze, and the forced marches in the Sudan. Gone, almost everywhere, were the long star-lit nights beneath Bedouin tents, in which the Englishman pleasantly deluded himself that his friendship with the Arab was something special, mutual and indestructible, and that there existed some affinity of spirit between the desert and the shires. The tough cheerful officers of the Sultan's private armies were among the last f their breed, still purveying the Small Arms Manual to illiterate peasants and tribesmen, and still managing to mould the most unlikely material into fine and faithful fighting forces. I liked them very much.

The two officers of the Batinah Force, dressed for the parade in impeccably pressed tropical uniforms, with medals and Sam Brownes, invited me into their mess for tea. A faint English aroma of tobacco, Brasso, leather, whisky and dogs hung about the stairs of their house; and it was like visiting an exhibition of Britain Abroad in some kind of pre-war Empire festival to sit in their soft arm-chairs at tea-time. There we were in the birth-place of Sindbad the Sailor, fresh from the ousting of the Imam from his capital at Nizwa, surrounded by the palm groves of the Batinah coast, on the shores of the Gulf of Oman; yet the commanding officer, carefully removing his Sam Browne, apologized for the weak tea and asked if I would care to try one of these little biscuits, they really were rather nice? English magazines and soldierly books lay about the room, and if there was not actually chintz around the windows, there was certainly a chintzy flavour to the *ménage*. A dog, and a beautiful sleek cat shared these quarters, which had no more in common with the oil camp at Fahud than they had with the proselyte's house at Ibri. From the big window, if you were careful with your tea-cup, and moved the copy of the Master of Belhaven's memoirs slightly to one side, and were adroit enough not to knock over the delicately-arranged vase of flowers which stood on the window-sill, you could see the Sultan's slaves cooking a goat over the camp-fire.

One of my hosts showed me a magnificent old Omani musket, five feet long, which he had picked up after the fight against Talib, at a town called Rostak. It was a warlike town, he said, where such things seemed natural enough, though the gun, blackened and rusty, did look rather strange propped up against the sofa. He told me that Talib had put up a brave resistance, and had still not been caught: rumour was strong that he had slipped away by boat from this very coast, but there had been no welcoming paeon from Saudi Arabia, where he would presumably take refuge. He had simply vanished, like a jinn, perhaps to fight another day; and so far as I know he has never been seen since, from that day to this. 'You have to confess a sneaking admiration for a chap like that,' said the major. 'He really put up quite a decent show.'

A young servant with a clown-like face took away the tea-things, but as he left the major, who had formerly been a Royal Marine, whistled a boatswain's call between his teeth. The servant at once put down his tray, and standing stiffly to attention in an irresistibly funny parody of the British naval manner, intoned in a strange nasal voice, rather like a ventriloquist: 'Do you hear there? Do you hear there? Cooks to the galley! Hands to make and mend clothes! Up spirits! Away first motor-boat's crew! Hands to muster on the quarter-deck!' before picking up his tray again with exaggerated gravity and leaving the room. 'I've taught him all the boatswains' calls,' said the major. 'Let me know if you want to hear some more.'

It looked plain sailing, on the map, from Sohar to the city of Muscat: but in fact it depended, oddly enough, upon the tides. If they were convenient we could drive all the way along the sands, for 100 miles or more: if not, we had to find our way through countless murky alleys among the palm trees. The former would be a delight; the latter an agony. In the event we tasted both. The soldiers advised us to wait until noon, when the tide would be right, and then set out along the sands: but the Sultan hated to waste a minute, so we spent most of the morning making what speed we could through the palm groves. It was the most trying and depressing part of our entire journey. The groves, which looked so lovely from the hills, and which did have a certain shadowy and haunting magic to them, began to feel intolerably confining. The tracks were thick with loose dust, kicked up by the hoofs of numberless camels, and we could only keep moving by dashing along them at high speed. The consequent clouds of dust hid almost everything from sight and covered us with a horrible grey mantle. Our route was intricate. Because, I suppose, of the quirks of the Moslem inheritance laws, the groves seemed to be divided in the most inconsequential way, and the tracks had to wind through the plantations quixotically, sometimes changing course at right angles, sometimes doubling back again, sometimes leaving the groves altogether for a mile or two and emerging on the beach or in the streets of some small seaside town. (*Bang! bang!* went the welcoming guns, as if they had been waiting all night for us, and the flags fluttered from the roof-tops.)

Before we were all exhausted, however, we moved on to the sands: and then away we sped like racing-drivers. The sand was wide, hard and level, and it stretched into the distance like a tape-measure, or some extravagant but unfrequented corniche. The drivers sang to themselves as they sped along, sometimes racing each other, only taking care to keep behind the Sultan and the big red flag. The slaves on the back hung on for their lives. The qadi clutched his turban. The goats had all been eaten. Often the spray splashed up over the windscreens and into the cabs, making our faces salty and sore. Sometimes we got stuck in a soft patch of sand. Once a truck suddenly careered so far off its course that I thought it would be swallowed into the sea, only to make a sudden swerve back again with a splashing of water and a chorus of shouts from the retainers. As we progressed we found that the nearer we were to the water, the harder was the sand: so soon we were driving actually through the shallows, driving the crabs helter-skelter up the sand, agitating the small fishes, and raising white plumes behind us. A few streams ran down to the sea from the mountains, and we had to probe a way through their channels, finding places shallow enough for us to cross. They cut deep courses in the sand, and one or two trucks were immured in them, the wet affecting their engines, until the slaves hitched up their skirts and leapt into the water to push from behind. But such mishaps as there were proved trivial and transient. The sun shone brightly on us all day; the sea was tranquil; our progress was swift and stimulating.

The coast, belying a pristine emptiness on my map, turned out to be heavily populated, and we roared past an almost continuous strip of fishing and date-growing villages, all of palm-frond huts. It looked rather like some immensely elongated Florida resort, not at the height of the season. Many of the people were Baluchis, and their women were dressed in dazzling orange gowns, with bright pantaloons showing beneath them. The men waved as we passed; the children scampered after us; and a multitude of savage dogs barked and bared their teeth and chased us along the sand. This had once been the pirate coast *par excellence* ('They are murderers and brigands every one,' said Sir John Malcolm of the Gulf Arabs in 1786.

'They are monsters') and it still had a piratical flavour. High-prowed fishing boats were lined up on the beaches, their long protruding stems looking exactly like rams, so that I found it easy to imagine them putting to sea with crews of cut-throats. In another kind of boat, made of open wicker-work, fishermen paddled about half in, half out of the water, their brown shoulders and chests sinister above the breakers. Here and there a crumbling fort glared at us across the sand. In the palm groves beyond the villages we could often see the dim, moving figures of camel-men, their rifles slung across their backs, like brigands in a forest. (I remembered an engraving I had once been shown of Sohar, from a drawing made by an officer during an expedition against pirates. The great fort was belching smoke. Half the town was afire. In one corner a ferocious mob of Arabs was advancing with drawn sabres, cutlasses, muskets, camels and scowling beards. In another a company of soldiers was drawn up steadfastly for battle, muskets at the ready. Offshore stood the warships, ensigns flying, their big guns firing with puffs of cottony smoke. 'Sohar,' said the caption blandly, in copper-plate script. 'A View from the South-East.')

Past the lines of Burastis we went; and past the town of Sib (where that significant treaty had been signed nearly forty years before); and past two desolate rocky islands off the shore; and over a bleak spur of the mountains, from where we could see the blue expanse of the Gulf shining away towards Persia: until at last we left the coastline and climbed into a shallow amphitheatre among rocky hills. We were on the doorstep of the city of Muscat, which lay shielded by a rampart of hills as a kitchen garden is cherished in red brick. We camped among drab brown rocks on harsh and stony ground, but we knew that the old seaport lay awaiting us just over the ridge. A little village of mud huts near our camp was lavishly decorated with flags and streamers, and from the neighbouring burastis there came the reedy music of a pipe, playing an air of celebration. The Sultan was back in his own country, Caesar home from

Britain. Tomorrow he would enter his capital in glory. It was well known that he did not much like wild festivities or pompous ceremonial; but his subjects, it appeared, were not going to miss such an opportunity for merry-making. 'Very, very good,' said my driver as the tents were pitched, thinking no doubt exclusively of his wife.

Not far away there stood a square fort, exactly like a toy one, guarding the way into the capital and commanding the whole of the enclosed plateau on which we were encamped. It was commanded by an English colonel from Lyme Regis, who lived in it with his wife, feeling like a character from the pages of *Beau Geste*. Its guns, trained to cover precisely the correct field of fire, dominated the plain. In its fortified courtyards were tabulated stocks of weapons and ammunition. Smart sentries patrolled its ramparts. It had its own workshops, married quarters and football field. I never saw such a neat and trim little fort, so complete and self-contained in every respect. But in Muscat and Oman every facet of life has its touch of the peculiar. In the evening the colonel took me to see the head of the falluj from which the garrison drew its water. As the sun went down, and I approached the well-like opening of this channel, a great grotesque wave of black flapping things soared out of it into the dusk. The bats of the fort were off to greet their Sultan.

8

A warning—into Muscat—Sultan's reception—twin ports—harems, slavery and disease—at night— farewell audience

'There's one thing I ought to warn you about Muscat,' said the Wazir as he drove me into the city, the tails of his turban streaming picturesquely in the breeze. 'You must never go out at night without a lantern. It's an absolute rule that in the evening nobody at all wanders about without one, and if you do you'll almost certainly spend the rest of the night in the gaol.'

'Probably a custom several centuries old,' I conjectured dreamily, 'from the days when Muscat ruled an empire, and traders and agents from distant capitals walked through its streets.'

'Not at all,' said the Wazir. 'It started a few years ago, when some ass of a Chinese seaman got himself into trouble one night.'

For such was the character of Muscat, perched in the place where the Omani mountains reached the sea, that quaint old traditions could not only be honoured: they could also very easily be instituted.

Into Muscat

We had left the Sultan behind, conferring with some of his officials, and were driving through a rocky defile towards the city. Small crows were beginning to gather here and there, and the road was blazing with flags, banners and huge slogans of loyalty. One burgher of vision had acquired a roll of pink satin from a haberdasher and fixed it to poles along the side of the road—fifty yards or more of unabashed slithery pinkness, such as housemaids used to wear to dances. Already little knots of people were dancing in the streets to hand-clapping and the music of pipes, and a forest of flags flew from the pinnacles of the incredible profusion of forts and battlements that guarded the approaches to the capital. Everyone knew the Sultan was coming home triumphantly, and if there were any who regretted the obliteration of the Imamate, they were discreet enough not to show it.

The road wound its way through difficult country, and it was easy to see how successfully (even before the days of the toy fort with the bats) Muscat could be defended. There had been many times in history when the tribes of the interior had been at war with the rulers of Muscat. Sometimes they had succeeded in taking and sacking the city: but generally their progress had been halted here, in this beetling pass above it. It was here that British troops fought the decisive battle of the 1913 rebellion. (The first British campaign in Oman, mounted in 1820 to support the Sultan against a revolt, ended disastrously, with the loss of 6 officers, 270 men and 22 guns, and had to be revenged with a second expedition.) Here, too, the Portuguese managed to hold their own in many a desperate battle before the Arabs finally broke their grip, engulfed Muscat, and ended Portuguese control of south-east Arabia. When the famous Turkish buccaneer Ali Beg stormed the city in 1581 he surprised its defenders by landing a force farther down the coast and springing upon Muscat from the rear, advancing through a pass in these hills 'so narrow that two men cannot pass it abreast; no one imagining that he would attempt it'. Though not high, the crags around us looked indeed almost impregnable to armies, and our road was always over-looked by forts and breastworks, like a frontier pass through the Alps. The Greek mariners called Muscat 'the hidden port' because it was so difficult to detect from the sea; but it was no less aloof when approached from its landward side.

Oddly enough, I recognized these approaches to the city, though to my knowledge I had never seen a photograph of Muscat in my life. Soon after the war a book was published by an Irishman, Raymond O'Shea, called *Sand Kings of Oman*, in which he described a visit to a ruined 'lost city', within the borders of the Empty Quarter, never seen by a European before. The geographers viewed this likeable if unconventional account with a certain scepticism: and I was inclined to agree with them when I realized with a start that Mr. O'Shea's illus-tration of his legendary city, which I had studied with respectful interest, indisputably showed our well-known road into Muscat. There is something almost Oriental about the glorious effrontery of the Irish.

The road dipped sharply into Muscat, and after passing a little settlement of burastis, and a big open space in which a dozen loaded camels sat gloomily ruminating, we passed through a great gateway in a city wall and found ourselves in the capital. I was not at all sure whether we were actually in Muscat, or in its twin seaport of Mattrah, lying adjacent, and anyway we drove so quickly, and the gay crowds so obliterated the scenery, that one street seemed to merge pretty inconclus-ively with the next. But I gained an immediate impression, on this original entry, of age and piquancy, about equally mixed. Everything seemed to be whitewashed or built of a whitish stone, making it a clean, pale, rocky sort of place. The dark hills rose above us; the flags on the forts gave the scene a sense of perpetual flickering motion; the clothes of the passers-by were vividly coloured; sometimes through narrow alleys I caught a glimpse of the sea. In a few minutes the fine carved doorway of the Wazir's house opened to admit us, and we toasted the Sultan, ourselves, the New Year and the Wazir's newly-born granddaughter in a bottle of excellent champagne.

Next morning there was a brief celebratory reception at the Sultan's palace, in a long white hall overlooking the harbour, at which the Muscatis arrived in force and in finery to congratulate their ruler. The Sultan had lingered for an hour or two in the hills outside, but from dawn onwards the crowds had been waiting in the street for him, dancing and singing, waving slogans and banners, shouting, laughing and singing monotonous country songs. I went to the palace with the Wazir, who was wearing a long black aba and a beret, making him look rather like an eccentric vice-chancellor of one of the ancient universities. We were greeted by a number of the Sultan's more prominent relatives, all very cheerful and friendly, one of them carrying a complex of three cameras slung around his shoulders. A guard of honour of the Sultan's fourth and last private army, the Muscat Rifles, was drawn up in the street outside, wearing pill-box hats. Pressing and boisterous was the crowd that morning, and when the Sultan finally arrived the crush entering the palace and going up its stairs was so great that two of my friends the slaves lifted me bodily by the armpits and carried me up, while the wildly pushing throng of Muscatis, cluttered with canes and accoutrements, looked on and laughed and gave a helpful shove or two.

In the reception-room, when once we had penetrated there, we found the usual solemnly-sitting rows of dignitaries, whispering to each other, and rising respectfully to their feet when the Sultan entered. We all bowed low; the Sultan seated himself upon a modest throne; and we entered upon that familiar half-hour of agonized fossildom, than which it would be difficult to conceive a more inadequate way of expressing joy and affectionate compliments. A strained hush fell upon the assembly as the servants moved around with padded footsteps, pouring coffee and distributing sweetmeats. I found myself next to a distinguished elderly Egyptian of the old school, wearing a tarboosh and a stiff white collar, who introduced himself as the head of the customs department. He said I was welcome to Muscat, and hoped I had enjoyed my journey with the Sultan, which he had heard all about. I asked him what he thought of the revolutionary régime in Egypt. He said cautiously that I probably knew as much about it as he did, but that if I would care to see anything of the Muscat customs or harbour departments I would be very welcome. I asked him if he thought the Saudis would react strongly to the Sultan's action. He replied that the date season had been disappointing. I said it was interesting to think that the whole of the Sultanate was now united under one authority. He said yes, and did I not think these sweetmeats were very agreeable? So our conversation, like that of most of our companions, languished, withered, and petered out: and we sat there silent and congealed like mummies, until the slave came around with the incense, and we wafted it over our faces fastidiously. 'It's really meant to sweeten the beard,' said my neighbour, 'but of course you haven't got one.'

Our journey was accomplished, our purpose achieved: but such a grand and unprecedented tour of the Sultanate would not have been complete without an investigation of Muscat, its ancient capital, of which Sir Ronald Storrs once wrote that nothing could be more Byronically picturesque. I was probably the first European to approach this place for the first time from the interior, for in normal times its only method of communication with the outside world was by sea. No trains came to Muscat, no long-distance buses, no regular air services. My arrival accordingly failed, in a most satisfactory way, to coincide with any means of getting out of the place again. There was no ship up the Gulf for some little time. The Sultan was not returning to Dhufar with his convoy until the spring. I settled down with satisfaction to explore a city so renowned to the ancients and so puzzlingly little known to the contemporary world. 'Go where you like,' said the authorities; 'come and say good-bye to the Sultan before you leave, and don't forget your lantern!'

They stood side by side, Muscat and Mattrah, in neighbouring rocky coves, like two old Arab merchantmen in adjoining berths. Only a protruding spit of land, crowned with fortifications, divided them, and they peered at each other over the intervening hills with a trace of crotchety jealousy. There were some cars in these cities, and a telephone system, and a little power house; a small English community sweated away the years there, and you could buy a camera film or a hair-net in the shops; once a week the steamer put in, on its way up the Gulf or back to India. Yet they remained the most leisurely, unspoilt and charming of the Arabian ports, untrammelled by noisy political aspirations, not yet smeared by the manicured finger of oil. They were gentle and friendly places, very different from the highlands we had just left, where violence was never far below the surface. (The blue range of the mountains could be seen above the hills of Muscat, and it was queer to think that until a week or two before they had been ruled by a separate authority, and might soon have become an independent kingdom.) They also felt cosy and sheltered, so neatly were they tucked away between the mountains and the sea; as if they were preserved in glass cases, or perhaps pickled.

The waterfront of Muscat was only two or three hundred yards long, squeezed in among rocks at the end of a long, narrow, crooked cove. So cramped was it that there was only room for eight or nine buildings on it, giving the ignorant traveller an erroneous impression of the size of the place. There was the comfortable house of the British Consul-General, with a big flag in its courtyard; the customs house; and the Sultan's palace, a fine square building that had once been the residence of the Portuguese governor, as well as his factory, chapel, warehouse and barracks. These structures stood there huggermugger, and frowned sternly down the cove. They were guarded by two imposing forts, one on each side. On the north was Fort Murani, begun by the Portuguese in the 1580s. It was a wonderful fairy-tale castle above the water, with three or four turrets, machicolated platforms, winding passages, loopholes, embrasures and great stone gateways. Old cannons lay about all over the place, some of them abandoned carriage-less, one or two still pointing fervently to sea, rusting but undaunted. One I examined bore the British crown and the date 1799. Others were seventeenth-century Portuguese pieces. There was a little round Catholic chapel, with a stoup for Holy Water and an Ave Maria carved above a window. When the Arabs took this stronghold in 1650 they only spared those members of the garrison who 'consented' to embrace Islam: a forgivable demand, for the Portuguese had razed half the mosques along that Muscat seaboard, and slaughtered or mutilated a large proportion of the population.

On the other side of the anchorage stood the big prison fortress of Jelali, called by the Portuguese São João. I recognized this citadel at once. Mr. O'Shea had a picture of it, with the sea lapping the rocks at its foot, splendidly captioned: 'An ancient fortress in the western Hajar mountains, once the home of the Sheikh of Kalba.' With its two strong round towers and the steep stone stairs which led to its barbican, Jelali looked as hard for convicts to get out of as it must have been for attackers to get in. Once a day the prisoners emerged from its gateway, I was told, and stumbled down the steps with petrol tins to fetch water; but when I climbed up there the only person to be seen was a stuttering janitor at the gateway, who stared at me pallidly as if I had risen from the sea itself, like a merman, and nervously refused me admission.

The anchorage guarded by these two brave forts was bounded by precipitous rock walls, and it had long been the custom for ships visiting Muscat to have their names inscribed on the rocks in white paint. Muscat had been familiar to the Royal Navy for many generations, at least since the first campaigns against the Arab pirate fleets, and it had always been in the thoughts of British naval commanders intent on maintaining the sea routes to India. Indeed, in the early 1800s Said ibn Sultan, most famous of the rulers of Muscat and Oman, actually presented a ship of the line to the British Admiralty (his own fleet included seventy-five warships, but it has been unkindly suggested that only one ship could be manned at a time.) Hundreds of naval names were therefore on the rocks, some of them freshly painted, some of them so faded by age and sunshine that you could barely make out their letters. There were innumerable good old British names like *Teazer* or *Surprise*, and several American and Indian ships were also represented; one inscription recorded a visit by H.M.S. *Hardinge*, the ship which hovered so effectively along the Arabian shore during the Arab Revolt, and which the Arabs thought must be peaceably inclined because she only had one funnel. I sympathized with the generations of midshipmen who had climbed those rugged rocks with their little painting parties, in the heat of the Muscat sun. (In the summer it was one of the hottest places on earth; a Persian visitor in 1442 reported that the gems in the handle of his dagger were reduced to coal by the heat, and the desert was filled with roasted gazelle.) It was all very well when the ship's name was *Swan*, *Fox*, or *Teal*, but imagine painting H.M.S. *Duchess of Edinburgh* on the bare rock in such an inferno! Some people thought the efforts of such resolute sailors had disfigured the captivating harbour of Muscat. I liked the inscriptions, for they reminded me of the Greek travellers who carved comments upon the Colossi of Memnos, at Thebes, and of the generations of explorers who cut their names upon the rock of El Morro in Mexico; and anyway an honest British naval name never disfigured anything. The Sultan liked them, too. He called the anchorage 'my visitors' book'. When I mentioned the poor midshipmen to him, he told me that Nelson had visited Muscat as a midshipman in 1775 and spent two months there, thereby missing the news of the Battle of Concord. Who knew? Perhaps he had himself climbed the rock to record the name of H.M.S. *Seahorse* (frigate, twenty guns). He was 'stout and athletic' then, according to Southey, and would have been admirable for the job.

There were two gaps or breaches in the eastern wall of the anchorage. One was a small isthmus with a sandy beach, on which in earlier centuries trading ships from China used to beach themselves; some Muscatis still called it Chinese Harbour. The other, a shallow, narrow channel between the rocks, linking the anchorage with the open sea, also had associations with the Far East. During the last war a Japanese submarine crept up to this gap from the outside, and, adroitly aiming a torpedo through it, sank a Norwegian merchantman lying inside the anchorage. It was perhaps the nearest that the two wings of Hitler's axis ever came to joining: the submarine commander, presumably refuelling from tankers in the Indian Ocean, must have sailed his ship at least 6,000 miles from base. When, during the Napoleonic wars, the British frigate *Concord* captured the French frigate *Vigilant* in the very same harbour, those commanders, too, were a longish way from home.

Few ships were to be seen inside the anchorage nowadays, but often enough you would hear the muffled beat of engines at sea, and look up in time to catch the long slim outline of a tanker passing the end of the cove; and sometimes a freighter would be standing off-shore enmeshed in a web of small boats, while the lighters and country craft ferried her cargo ashore. Mattrah was the capital's mart and merchant centre, where the Indian importers lived in their fine seaside houses, and the big bazaar was crammed with merchandise. From Mattrah the camel caravans set off into the mountains; and there the cargoes from the ships were stocked in antique warehouses and checked by the minions of my tarbooshed Egyptian from the customs department. The dark suks, roofed with palm-fronds and lined with dim open-fronted shops, were always crowded with visiting bucolics, sweaty and swarthy. When I went there to buy a pair of sandals I came across a party of our Bedouin, confidently led by that old scoundrel the guide, who said his toothache was better but now complained of a strange stabbing sensation in the roof of his mouth; they were looking around like schoolboys on a half-term treat, and most willingly advised me on my purchase (to the chagrin of the shopkeeper, who quite rightly thought me easy meat). Muscat, home of Sultans, Consul-Generals, Wazirs and Muscat Rifles, had a reserved, St. James's-like flavour to it, characterized by grave sages telling their strings of beads: but Mattrah, down the road, was a bustling, shifting, cheery, money-making, barefoot, cross-legged kind of place, where the camel-men spent a night or two before trekking back into the mountains, and the Arab sailors lounged on their old sailing-boats in the bay.

I strolled along the beach at Mattrah one morning to watch the fishermen selling their catches. Now and again a very old car came rattling along the sands, for it was quicker than mani-pulating a passage through the tortuous alley-ways of the town: but the people continued their business undisturbed, the crowds of gay-costumed Baluchi women arguing shrilly beside the boats, the fishermen, grey and wrinkled, shouting out their offers, the dumpy children playing with shells and flotsam. One man offered me a small shark, a fish highly regarded by the Muscatis (they eat part of it, dry part of it, and send the fins to China); another was anxious to sell me a swordfish. On a fishing boat near the shore, gently dipping and rolling, a solitary cadaverous ill-shaven Arab was standing with his arms stretched along the cross-spar, as if crucified: his face was wicked but haunting, and he stood there slowly moving with the rocking of the boat, in a long black gown with rents in it, backwards and forwards, up and down, like a gaunt tortured figure from Goya.

This interesting beach was lined with houses, some of them joyously gimcrack, with toppling balconies and shaky windows, some of them grand and well-preserved. I came across a big archway among these buildings, leading into a courtyard; and since there seemed to be fairly constant move-ment in and out of it I stepped across its threshold. At once two or three Arabs standing by (one of them selling pink and yellow combs) jumped to my side and warned me that it was a harem entrance. It looked very large, said I. It was, said they. There must be a very large number of wives inside it, I said. That was as may be, they replied. Could I just peep around the corner? I wondered. On the whole, they thought, no. I could see a little of the courtyard anyway, by pressing myself close to the wall; but there were no henna'd houris inside, only two or three drab women who seemed to be doing the laundry, more like Mrs. Mopp than Aimee Dubucq. Nevertheless, though Muscat was as much an Indian or Baluchi city as an Arab one, the harem was still a lively and powerful institution, and its inmates were still jealously guarded from intrusion. The Sultan's own mother was closeted in her house, an intelligent and agreeable recluse; and many other Arab ladies only saw the city when they scurried after dark, with their lanterns, from one high mansion to another.

'Are there slaves in there?' I asked the man who was selling combs. He said there were not, and indeed I think slavery was probably dead in those twin cities, though most of its many negro inhabitants were descendants of freed men. In the days when both the French and the British governments were working against slavery in the Persian Gulf the freed men of Muscat used to call themselves 'British' or 'French', according to the consulate that had secured their release, and formed devoted factional clubs, assiduously celebrating their respective national days and sometimes reflecting, as if in microcosm, whatever Anglo-French squabble then happened to be raging. Since British influence had become paramount in the Gulf there had only been a British representative in Muscat (the American consulate closed in 1915), and the Consul-General still sometimes obtained freedom for slaves who had escaped from their masters in the interior and travelled to Muscat to clasp the consulate flagstaff—the traditional way of demanding manumission. I hung around the Consulate courtyard once or twice in the hope of witnessing this archaic drama; but no tattered negroes rushed into the yard as I loitered there, and none of those who passed by bore the chains or whip-scars of servitude.

Slavery was, of course, still rampant elsewhere in the

Arabian peninsula, often in its worst forms. Later that year the United Nations considered ways of preventing slave traffic in the Indian Ocean, the Persian Gulf and the Red Sea, through which numbers of negro slaves were reaching Saudi Arabia. According to some reports, a few of these unfortunates were actually shipped through Muscat, and some were still smuggled to Riyad via Buraimi, or at least were until the British took control of the oasis. Since the Saudis did not see anything reprehensible in slavery, and had plenty of money to spend, it is easy to appreciate that the Muscati middlemen must have been tempted to dabble in this lucrative trade: and perhaps they did.

The Sultan certainly kept his own household slaves in Dhufar, some of whom had been our lively companions on the journey: but I am told that his lenient attitude towards them, and his opposition to the crueller aspects of slavery, had made him unpopular among some of the slave-masters of the penin-sula. His own slaves, for example, were not only well fed and generally kindly treated, but even (in some cases) went home in the evenings like commuters. Slaves serving in his private army were given week-end leave. Some were paid wages, and old men were often pensioned. Some, granted manumission, preferred to remain in the Sultan's service anyway. If a slave married a slave woman, their children became slaves by divine dispensation; but if a slave married a free woman, the Sultan did not claim the offspring. The palace slaves enjoyed no sinecure (I gathered that if they did not shave their heads they were whipped) but it would be wrong indeed to think of them as enduring perpetual miseries or privations. They had all the advantages of the welfare state, with one exception: they had to work.

Anyway, as an evil slavery was insignificant in Arabia com-pared with disease. Not far from my beach was the American mission hospital of Mattrah. Patients laboured hundreds of miles from the interior to be treated at this place, and its rooms were crowded with poor ragged scabrous families, who did

130

their best to recreate there some semblance of their homes: for if a man was sick he brought his wife and children to hospital with him, and they did their washing, cooking, crying and squabbling beside his sick-bed. Some years before the head of this mission had visited the interior to give some medical help to the then Imam, Ghalib's predecessor, and by keeping his eyes open and taking many photographs he had returned perhaps the best-informed authority on that practically unknown territory. By 1955 he had left Muscat, but I heard a great deal about him, one appealing (if unconvincing) suggestion being that he had really penetrated the mountains on behalf of the American oil interests in Saudi Arabia. 'Just like you,' said someone. 'Don't tell me you made that journey with the Sultan just to *write* about it!'

The hospital was a big brick building in a compound, close beneath the hills, well but modestly equipped and run by a tiny staff of devoted American nonconformists. They took me to see their leper colony, inhabited by an incorrigibly cheerful community, men and women, enjoying their happiest days for many years: there within the compound they could live their cloistered lives with some degree of dignity, no longer reviled, stoned, driven away or denounced as inimical agents of darkness. The Americans had managed to dispel, to an astonishing extent, any sense of the pariah or the uncanny. The doctors shook hands readily with the lepers, only being careful to wash thoroughly when they had left the compound; and the inmates waved good-bye gaily and affectionately when we walked away. I found it an elating experience. Much worse to see, for the layman, were the unhappy sufferers from trachoma, one of the scourges of Arabia. In this appalling disease the eyelashes are so turned inwards that they are constantly brushing against the eyeballs, causing indescribable pain and discomfort. It is curable, if treated early enough, but outside Muscat there was scarcely a doctor in the whole of the Sultanate, and everywhere men peered at you with eyes distorted and watering from trachoma. It is possible to look at a leper without a spark of fellow feeling, and only the most detached kind of compassion, for the slow decaying of limbs is something totally alien to our circumstances: but everyone knows what it is like to have an eyelash in one's eye. 'We could fix both these diseases', said one of the doctors, 'if we had the money. There's no leprosy in England any more, and precious little trachoma. If we could isolate all the lepers, and treat all these poor guys with trachoma from the start, we could probably do away with them both here. But of course it all needs money, and plenty of it.'

'Oil money, perhaps,' I said.

He shrugged his shoulders and smiled. Any old money would do.

Promptly at eight in the evening the big gun went off from the battlements of Murani, and the heavy wooden gates of Muscat were closed. Like a city of Europe in the Middle Ages, the capital settled down to a night behind walls, and nobody could enter or leave it. The Wazir's servant handed me my flickering lantern as I left the house to walk about the city, and asked solicitously if I would like him to accompany me. I assured him I would be safe enough, but he followed me all the same, and for half an hour or so as I wandered about I could see *his* flickering little lantern keeping at a discreet distance behind me, stopping when I stopped, starting when I started, wavering when I wavered, and only leaving me when it seemed to be, on the whole, improbable that I was about to be set upon by robbers. The people of Muscat were a kindly lot, and often performed such unobtrusive acts of courtesy.

There was something soothing and magical about that old city at night, after so many days of virile and stately excitement. There was a little of Jerusalem to its *mystique*, a little of Charleston, just a touch of the back streets of Oxford, a trace of one of those little fishing ports on the Gulf of Venice—and the whole welded and illumined by an overpowering sense of the old Arabia, compounded of ships, lattice windows and hidden influential ladies. Few street lights illuminated the crooked little alleys, and only a few passers-by swung their lanterns,

swished their garments and wished each other mellifluously:
'Peace be with you!' In the crevices of the suk one or two shops
were open, and the merchants sat cross-legged beside their
shutters, and oil lamps shone softly among the bottles or bales
of fabric. A hush was on the city. In the gatehouse in the walls a
few askaris lay asleep on benches, and the announcements of
ships' arrivals ('Mails to be Aboard by Nine-Thirty Sharp')
flapped in the gentle breeze from the sea: rows of rifles hung
neatly on the walls, many of them colourful with bright blue,
red and green plastic slings, bought from Indian merchants in
the bazaar. Down a devious lane I glimpsed four veiled
shadowy figures hurrying towards the quayside, at once furtive
and sheepish, led by a white-robed servant of grand physique.

High above the harbour (as I wandered along the sands,
sheltering my lamp against the wind) the two big forts shone
dimly. A ghost of an Arab dhow was in the anchorage. I
crossed the little isthmus to the harbour of the Chinamen, and
looked out past the rocks to the Indian Ocean. Imprinted in the
soft sand was a single large footprint, its toes clearly defined,
like a one-legged Man Friday's. Small crabs rustled away into
the sea-weed. From the ramparts of Murani, behind me, there
echoed the sad quarter-tones of a sentry's song. The sea looked
cold but sentimental.

I turned, the crabs scuttling from my footsteps, and strolled
back along the sand. The servant had long since left me, and I
was all alone beside the anchorage. A few lights shone from the
high houses of the town, with their shuttered windows and ponderous carved doors, and the generator of the little power house
thumped away busily through the darkness. It was a night of
infinite serenity, in a city lovingly protected against the on-
slaughts of worldliness. All the sheikhs, cannons, bare deserts,
coffee pourers, flags, roaring engines, clamours, rifle-shots,
animals and oil wells of our journey seemed no more than
distant and unlikely memories; and since no lamp burned from
the windows of the Sultan's palace, I assumed that indefatig-
able potentate to be fast asleep.

Before I went to say good-bye to him, in the morning, I listened to the wireless news to hear what the world thought of his adventures in Oman. 'I wonder how familiar you are', he had asked me in Salala, 'with the map of south-east Arabia?' Totally unfamiliar I had been, and blissfully unfamiliar most of the world remained. Important issues had been at stake in the mountains, having their bearing on empires, corporations and hoary dynasties: but the citizen of the West was no wiser about Nizwa or the Treaty of Sib than he had been when we embarked upon our adventure. Our travels had entered the news for a day or two, and the baffled reader learnt that the Imam had been dislodged; but the sands of news sift quickly, and any blurred impressions our affairs had made soon faded and dissolved and were swept away by the tide of greater (or more dazzling) events. A sentence or two in the news was sufficient to tell our story, sandwiched between a disarmament conference and the football results.

The Sultan, when the Wazir and I climbed the stairs to his private audience room, was therefore a lesson in relativity, for he gave the unmistakable impression of having just dictated a page of history. It would probably, in a generation or two, be all but indistinguishable from many other pages of the Muscati chronicles, for the past of this turbulent country was a constant laceration of punitive expeditions, civil wars, triumphant marches, reconquests, raids, assassinations and plunderings. ('The history of Oman', remarks one chronicler, 'affords few instances of the ruler returning from a journey without having to crush insurgents.') Nevertheless, for the first time in the present century Muscat firmly ruled the interior, and the Sultan sat in his gilded chair in an aura of victorious satisfaction.

He was not in his autocratic mood, and his eyes had lost the fiery pride that had so illuminated some of the ceremonies on the road: instead they had a soft, thoughtful, almost sleepy look beneath their heavy eyelids, reminding me rather of an elaborately turbanned Cheshire Cat. The Wazir, wearing his academic aba, bowed professionally, and I, feeling somewhat *in statu pupillari* beside him, clumsily did likewise: for there was something very formal about the Sultan's demeanour, now that he was sitting so snugly in his palace. We sat on a pair of ornate spindly chairs, directly in front of the Sultan, as if we were going to have our eyes tested, and I thanked him for allowing me to make the journey with him. He said he was very glad I was able to come, and would look forward to reading my account of it. He hoped I had been well treated during our travels? His servants had looked after me? The food was adequate? The tent had been comfortable? That was good.

We sipped sweet black coffee and talked of politics a little, but I no longer felt quite at home with this benignly smiling sovereign, friendly though he was. Serene and settled was his deportment now, and regally assured his manner: but I rather prefer my pleasures dry, Kirsch on my strawberries and my Sultans in Oman. For me Said bin Taimur would always remain a fawn-dressed travelling Sultan, a navigator, an Arab adventurer: and in memory I should always see him sitting in the cab of his truck, his sunglasses on his nose, checking a map distance between his finger and his thumb, or delving in his plastic-lined shopping bags to pull out a thermometer; while the convoy bumped and jolted its way across the Jeddat al Harasis, the Bedouin guide biting his lip in the front truck, and the big red flag streaming.

Through the window of the room I could see down the anchorage to the sea; and there stood the white ship which was to take me up the Gulf. We drained the coffee; inhaled the incense; shook hands with the Sultan; bowed again; and withdrew. As we walked together down the street the Wazir remarked to me gently: 'There's something I'd like to tell you about that interview, if you don't mind. I know you won't be hurt. In talking with these Arab rulers it's considered bad etiquette to sit with your legs crossed, as you were doing. Of course it didn't matter in the least—what really gives offence is when people sit in such a way that the *sole* of the shoe faces the ruler, if you understand me—you weren't doing that at all. But I thought you might like to be told. You never know, something of this kind might crop up in your life again one of these days.'

I looked back at the handsome square palace, with a sentry outside its gate and two cannons standing stoutly beside the wall, all very sedate and historical.

'I see,' said I, and we climbed into the Wazir's jeep.

Envoi

Sure enough, oil was found at Fahud (though not in the hole we inspected, and not by the oilmen we met). The Sultan did not, however, enjoy his revenues for long. His quaint brand of obscurantist paternalism, so beguiling to me during our short acquaintance, was not universally popular among his diseased, ignorant and poverty-stricken subjects, and the advent of oil monies meant that sooner or later he was bound to go. He was not murdered or tried for Crimes against the People (though some of his Dhufar soldiers did once try to assassinate him): no, he was quietly pushed off his throne by his worldly son Qabus, and died in exile in England in 1972.

The money began to flow in the 1960s, and within a decade the country was transformed. There was a slight renewal of trouble, it is true, from the recalcitrant Ghalib and Suleiman bin Hamyar, and a running war had to be fought against incursions from Communist South Yemen, to the west, but in general progress was uninterrupted. Even the name of the country was changed—it became simply Oman, symbolizing the unity our journey had so theatrically sealed—and the schools, hospitals, roads and hotels so neglected by Said bin Taimur were now erected at last. So absolutely were the barriers removed that before long there were direct flights from Europe to that lantern-lit seaport of the lepers and the twilight gun, Muscat.

The British connection was maintained, long after the end of Empire, and in 1979 the Queen of England paid a State visit to Oman. She was taken by car to Nizwa, where our journey had been consummated 22 years before: but no doomed goats swayed in the back of her vehicle, no big black slaves swathed like mummies against the sand, and no neat, plump, autocratic little Sultan, compass open on his lap, led the royal convoy up the wadi.

The past had vanished like a dream: and like a painted dream, half a lifetime on, does our own progress across Oman seem to me today.

Index